Living Modern Tropical

A Sourcebook of Stylish Interiors

490 color illustrations

Richard Powers Text by Phyllis Richardson

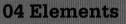

Living Modern Tropical copyright © 2012
Thames & Hudson Ltd, London
Text copyright © 2012 Phyllis Richardson
Photographs copyright © 2012 Richard Powers

Designed by Anna Perotti

First published in 2012 in hardcover in the United States of
America by Thames & Hudson Inc., 500 Fifth Avenue,
New York, New York 10110

thamesandhudsonusa.com

Library of Congress Catalog Card Number 2012932511

ISBN 978-0-500-51640-9

Printed and bound in China by Toppan Leefung Printing Ltd

Introduction

A warm breeze, swaying palms, a crystalline blue inlet mirrored by a perfect cerulean sky – these are the images and colours that are charged with the seductive allure of the tropics. It would be easy to reason that, given the modernist sensibility, in which ornament is pared down and a rational approach prefigures every design decision, the tropical aesthetic would defy the very essence of the approach.

But the truth is that a modern aesthetic can be applied to just about any decorative leaning, and the sense of balance, proportion, space and light used to singular

effect in an atmosphere where the natural environment is so sensuously potent. In fact, the more clean-lined and restrained the architecture, the more subservient it becomes to the richness of the natural environment and the more brilliant the contrast.

A clean white villa shadowed by arching palms and screened by blossoming frangipani has a particularly luxurious presence, the rectilinear insertion being softened by greenery, and the white-washed finish becoming a pure backdrop for a subtle range of hues. The coconut palm itself, with its linear trunk and bushy top, can be read as the happy

marriage of stark and lush that the modernist building in the tropical setting conveys. But as with the more general spectrum of modern approaches, the contemporary tropical hybrid produces many shoots that question ideas of what is modern, and the ways the definition expands with new possibilities.

The first house to be described in detail in English literature was a tropical concoction, the fortified enclosure constructed by the shipwrecked diarist Robinson Crusoe in Daniel Defoe's eponymous novel. A roughly built hut made from the flotsam of the sea and the natural

resources to hand, it became (through the story, if not the actual reading of the book) the inspiration for every child's own woodland den or tree-house habitat. And still the idea of creating a house from nature, in nature, open to the four winds but sheltering, comforting and satisfying, is a model for many electing to put up a house in the tropics. They are not seeking to build from sticks and driftwood, of course, but to have a house that embodies some of the elemental spirit of the handmade hut. Some of the houses in these pages accomplish this direct connection by making themselves

open to the natural environment, others by using massive, uninterrupted glass walls that make every surrounding spray and shrub part of the interior decor.

Perhaps it is the other end of the spectrum from the survivalist shelter and glass-walled, 'nature-orientated' house, but the most significant association between modern design and the tropical setting will be the striking mid-century creations by Oscar Niemeyer in Brasilia, a demonstration that the pure planes and materials of Modernism were at home in the lushness of the subtropical highland. Niemeyer's

legacy is seen here in the brilliant, low-lying white-washed villas and in the space-age, spherical hillside construction, with its clinical white interiors, that makes the most of its alien presence in the landscape.

And then there are the traditional, or even historic, colonial houses, with their colourful walls, arched openings and carved wood details. These, too, are part of the modern approach to tropical, made even more so by the works of Sri Lankan architect Geoffrey Bawa, when they balance ornament with simplicity, artificial and natural hues, light with shade, openness with shelter. The

architects featured here do not mimic Niemeyer, Bawa, or even Crusoe, but the lineage from simple hut to modern house can be traced to many of the following designs.

The modern house in a tropical environment must function well, just as a house in an alpine or desert setting must provide a comfortably livable atmosphere in those conditions. But the tropics demand less, in the sense that there needs to be some permeation of the elements to make the house work. Issues of ventilation, direct sunlight and plentiful rain all require a house to be open, elevated, unsealed. So there

are certain aspects of modernist design that, although they may have originated in cooler European climates, lend themselves perfectly to the tropics. The open-plan interior allows for the crucial circulation of air and light. A large overhanging roof provides a sheltered outdoor living area, shaded from the blazing sun but open to the fresh air. With the addition of a spacious porch or terrace, the open-plan arrangement makes it easier to enjoy the indoor–outdoor lifestyle that a warm climate inspires. Large sections of glazing make the lush vegetation part of the interior, and take

maximum advantage of a beautiful natural setting. The simplicity of a modernist building that focuses on a few well-chosen materials has a more immediate connection to the surroundings, especially when those materials are taken from or reflect the local natural resources.

In looking at how to 'live modern' in the tropics, it is helpful to consider the different elements or effects. Here we have divided these into chapters that consider the following: Nature, Water, Architecture, Elements, Light, Function, Furniture, Details, Materials and Outdoors. Within each chapter are the specific details that contribute to the overall appeal of a house and its interior. The 'tropics' are defined as the region that surrounds the equator. Moving from west to east, this would include, roughly, Central America and the northern parts of South America, including Colombia, Venezuela and Brazil, the Caribbean Islands and West Indies, central Africa and southern India, Southeast Asia, Indonesia and the Philippines, northern Australia, Papua New Guinea and various islands in the mid-Pacific. For our purposes, we have expanded the definition to include areas of the subtropics, such as more southern parts of the US and Australia, as well as one or two examples from north Africa and the Mediterranean.

When Robert Louis Stevenson wrote of leaving San Francisco and travelling towards Samoa, which would become his island home, he described feeling 'delightedly conscious. Day after day the air had the same indescribable liveliness and sweetness. I was aware of a spiritual change; or perhaps, a molecular reconstitution. My bones were sweeter to me.' So we modernists go to the tropics, in search of that something sweeter.

Nature

Setting
Integration
Views
Plants

In a tropical setting, the natural surroundings are understandably a primary influence on the character of a house, whether it is set in the thick growth of the rainforest, or a hillside above an ocean of swaying greenery, or huddled in an inlet, where the steady push and pull of the tide signals the calm passing of time. The sheer scale of tropical flora can appear overwhelming, but that is part of the appeal. And as the modern house has the intention of creating a receptive backdrop to the essential requirements of its inhabitants, the role of nature in the tropics goes almost without saying.

The vegetation of the rainforest represents the richness of life on Earth, and emphasizes our symbiotic relationship with the natural world. As the Mexican economist and politician Carlos Salinas de Gortari once put it, 'a single tree in the tropical forest in the south of Mexico has more different species than some European countries'. Ignoring any inherent criticism of Europe, one cannot help but be awed by the varieties and spectacle of tropical vegetation to which he refers.

Even those of us who have yet to travel in the tropics are familiar with a certain pulsing beauty associated

with the region. Perhaps we know it through films: the jungles of Vietnam or Indonesia from modern war cinema; the life teeming within the majestic canopy, hundreds of feet above the ground, through television documentaries. We've seen the silhouette of the twisted mangrove tree as it roots to the muddy river bottom; the banana tree, with its massive, paddle-like leaves; the bird of paradise; the fragrant frangipani; the ferns that form a lacy filter for the equatorial sun. Then there are the bolder colours of hibiscus, orchids, *caladium* ('elephant ear'). In a world where we can import even the most

exotic species to our own greenhouses, we have perhaps less appreciation for what the tropical climate offers in terms of its biodiversity. But one has only to encounter these species 'in the wild' to realize what this specialized region brings to the planet.

As for those who have the opportunity to live in this environment, the place of nature in the scheme of their own lifestyle and design is an important consideration. While the surroundings may not seem to require much thought, there are different approaches to making nature a genuine part of the living experience. The tropical home derives almost as much of its ambience from the surroundings as from any design feature. So plants will be bigger, more dominating, offering shade and sculptural forms to the interior, as well as the habitable outdoor spaces.

The framing of the view is also a part of the tropical house, since there is likely to be a particular vantage point over water or a valley, or even through dense forest, though it is likely to be a much less formalized sightline than one might find in a more traditional European house. We also consider the way that a tropical house, the interior and the structure, might integrate with the natural environment. This integration refers to the way in which the vegetation is allowed to grow inside the house or within its 'outdoor rooms', or the way that greenery outside becomes part of the interior through the use of large glass walls and doors.

Finally, the relationship between the modern tropical house and its environment is everything to do with the setting itself, the way the house is placed within the lush embrace of the jungle, or set apart from but still very much connected to the natural surroundings.

01

Some consider the word 'tropical' merely to imply a setting, like a stage set, rather than something that has a real effect on a building and its interiors. It is a word that too often suggests a passive condition, as if any house dropped down amid palms and mangroves will become somehow tropically inspired. But the setting is part of a relationship that the house has with its environment – how it is 'set' within the landscape, as much as what surrounds it. And setting is about whether it lies hidden by foliage, within a verdant embrace or set high above the treeline so that the inhabitants always have a clear idea of their place in nature. Below, houses in Australia use upper-level wooden decks to extend the reach of the living space into the trees. Opposite, the well-tended garden of a house in Sri Lanka flows into the natural vegetation.

Setting

Opposite, top, houses in Australia and California are partly obscured by the landscape. Opposite, bottom, left to right, a house by Frank Lloyd Wright in California uses native plants to complement the design of the concrete blocks; in Sri Lanka, a house is set like a summer pavilion in a clearing; and a modern-block house in Rio de Janeiro projects from the covering of the hillside. Below, a coastal California home offers a cliffside observation point. Following pages: a cool modern house in Bangkok by Duangrit Bunnag rises with, but not above, the surrounding trees.

01

Integration

It seems such a technical word for such a natural and enveloping experience. Where plants, trees, hedges and grasses, in untended surroundings or carefully arranged into planters, become not just a part of the setting of a house, but also essential to its overall ambience, even elements of its decor, it means a fluid integration. Opposite, in a modern Australian house the indoor–outdoor character is inherent owing to the continuous poured-concrete floor. A gap in the floor is given over to a shallow pool planted with grasses and water lilies. Above left, another Australian example brings not just planting, but also the elemental solidity of the rocks and boulders left exposed in a basement stairway, while in a California hillside house, above, middle, the neat zig-zag of a brick stair hardly interrupts the lush greenery. Another multi-level house in Brazil, above right, features a sculptural stair that weaves a delicate ribbon through mature trees and plants.

01

Integration doesn't always mean that a house is completely open to its surroundings, but at this house in Brazil, right, the designers have worked hard to achieve that fluidity. Both elevations feature massive glazed doors, which can be pulled to one side to create oversized openings to the generous decked terraces. They can also be closed up tightly against wind and rain. Another house in São Paulo, below, makes mature trees and water part of the interior environment. The trees sit beyond the roof overhang, but are enclosed with the house by the outer wall.

01

Outdoor spaces benefit from being well integrated with the natural environment, too. Above left, a Sri Lankan house includes outbuildings and an entrance gate and pathway that draw visitors inside, and also create welcoming spaces outside. Above middle, designer George Cooper's house in Sri Lanka combines a series of pavilions, so that walking among them, visitors encounter the jungle on three sides. Above right, the deck and pool of this modern Brazilian residence seem to merge with the surrounding greenery. Opposite, a house in Sri Lanka designed by Prabhakorn Vadanyakul features upper-floor deck space, where residents can sit up high to escape the heat and catch a fresh breeze.

01

Everyone wants a room with a view. But in the brilliance of a tropical paradise, it may be a case of being spoiled for choice. A good modern design, however, will capitalize on a stunning view to frame a nature scene or draw the eye to an unobstructed bright horizon. One drawback of some older, more traditional houses is that the need for ventilation and perhaps shade and thermal protection was considered much more important than a beautiful vista, which could be enjoyed immediately upon stepping out the door. But the modern tropical house will take the views even as a starting point, or at least as an imperative for the public spaces. Left, a house in Australia designed by Elizabeth Watson Brown frames the view over the pool and beyond from the comfortable shaded deck terrace. Below, a more exposed position at a beach house on the Gulf of Thailand.

Views

01

A house set in the subtropical hills of Southern
California provides living-room loungers with a
clear, seaward perspective over low-growing,
indigenous scrub. Opposite, this coastal retreat
on the eastern seaboard of Australia features a
protected walkway that focuses the view out
towards the bay and the mountains beyond.
Following pages, left, for a house perched above
Byron Bay, architect Sharon Fraser wrapped a
series of stark, modern planes around each
glorious sightline, and bathing takes on a new
meaning in this open-sided room in Bali, right,
from where the lap pool cleverly extends the
gaze through an antique timber gateway to the
jungle valley.

01

Plants

Ample vegetation is synonymous with 'tropical'. Gone are the days when Westerners attempted to 'tame' the landscape or turn bits of jungle into a corner of their European homeland. Native plants are not only a wonder to look at and discover, they also provide important shade, and help to cool temperatures and make the connection to the natural landscape that most people who move to the tropics are keen to exploit. In this modern Brazilian home, the greenery looks naturally abundant, but has been carefully sculpted to complement the building layers and elements. Following pages, left, this house in a northern suburb of Sydney could be an exotic island retreat, set behind plentiful ferns and gnarled eucalyptus; right, elsewhere, plants both native and new are used to screen patios, courtyards and an open dining area. Bottom left, a wall of greenery in a California garden encloses a cool, lush outdoor living space.

01

Water

02

Swimming pools
Reflecting pools
Ponds
Natural

The idyllic appeal of the tropics is generally defined by two elements: sunlight and water. Other details – a sandy beach, swaying palms, a spot for lounging, a romantic vista – can be exchanged for other amenities. But sun and water are necessary, elemental. Even the most conventionally designed house becomes an exotic retreat when perched beside a tropical sea, a secreted inlet, a gurgling stream. When dense foliage dampens the sound of trickling water or an open beach echoes with the crash of waves, the environment gains sensory dimension that bespeaks the cleansing cycles of nature. Water creates a tropical atmosphere through sound, through the view of a widening river or a tumbling sea, and through the taste of salty, moisture-rich air. Humidity is not something that many people crave, but the abundance of water all around is a tangible signal of the tropics. Cut with a freshening breeze, the humid condition can become intoxicating.

Ever since Frank Lloyd Wright positioned Fallingwater almost within the cascading falls, modern architecture has brought buildings much closer to the source. Of course, Islamic architecture has expressed this kind of harmony for centuries, pumping water indoors to bring the soothing natural tones of flowing water to an interior suited for quiet and meditation. Modern architecture has adopted some of this thinking, along with elements that derive from much earlier influences, such as the terraces of fountains and contemplative pools in the Shalimar Gardens in Lahore. Reflecting pools, with crisp, modern geometries or more organic forms have become an important part of planned garden spaces. Pools for swimming or reflecting have moved from backyard amenities to indoor–outdoor features.

Not merely a peaceful or soothing fixture, water also adds dynamism and excitement. The living space that overlooks an ocean or a river offers a constant source of movement and change, just as foliage – especially when viewed through generous windows – presents a continually evolving pattern of light and shade. Being in close proximity to a natural body of water also has a profound effect on the feel of a house, emphasizing the force of nature up against man-made boundaries.

Some designs emphasize those boundaries more than others. A house, like that in the jungle of Sri Lanka, sits close on the shore of the lake, with part of the building even hanging over the water, reminiscent of medieval bridge houses. Another, in Bali, features a swimming pool that flows beneath the porch canopy and appears to fall over the hillside into the verdant landscape below. But there is another approach to water features that favours a sharper distinction between the natural and the man-made, where pools become clearly marked-out parts of the hardscaping and the natural surroundings are very much the soft background to both the indoor and outdoor spaces. These are the sharp-edged modern houses in white-washed or natural concrete, with outside spaces that extend the living areas in distinctive linear forms.

As light and water play equal parts in the tropical atmosphere, the challenge is to design in concert with both, creating a structure that takes maximum advantage of natural lakes, rivers or streams and makes its own cooling ambience through shade and water. Modern design encompasses the thoughtful juxtaposition of these tropical elements, letting water become a gift to the senses.

Swimming pools

Even though a house and garden might be sited next to a natural and beautiful body of water, the desire for a private, well-designed feature is pervasive in the tropics. And the design continues to change and improve. The swimming pool has come indoors and gone out again. It has evolved in shape, size and colour. It has lost its defined edges, with designs that let water flow beyond the rim and into discreet drains, and gained an edge in sharp, modern forms, such as the crescent shape cut out around this circular terrace in California, left. In tropical environments, swimming pools are framed by tamed greenery, as in the Brazilian house seen on the previous pages, or designed to flow over the hillside, creating their own, free-flowing waterfall, as in the Balinese house, opposite.

The clear blue rectangle of indulgence is an
open-air experience in Marrakech, opposite,
where a tidy lawn contrasts with the smooth
concrete terrace to create a pattern of textures.
In the absence of leafy coverage, a pool house
provides a retreat from the harsh afternoon sun.
Above left, placing the long lap pool right up
next to a boundary wall overhung with trees in
the south of France gives swimmers a portion of
shade. Above, a house in California designed by
the revered modernist architect Craig Ellwood
centres the pergola on the width of the wide
pool. More symmetry, above right, in Brazil,
where the pool matches the low-profile linearity
of the main house. Following pages: in
Morocco, the pool terrace serves as an outdoor
dining space. A changing area is at right.

02

These pages offer a shadier perspective, in which the landscaping and the natural growth are brought up closer to the water. Below, a house in Colombo features a pool lined in emerald-green tiles, set within a cool, private courtyard. A row of palms in planters screens the concrete wall and makes the space more inviting. Below right, a pool in California makes a virtue of the narrow plot. Opposite, a slender lap pool in a modern Sri Lankan house is channelled around a planted 'island'. Following pages: in Sydney, left, a pool terrace features a bridge of sandblasted glass set flush in a pavement of smooth concrete; right, bamboo, grasses and a native pine soften the edges of a modern house and pool in California.

02-

Whether it is because there is not enough space for a proper swimming pool, or because there is some other inspiration for making water a calming feature, the reflecting pool can also add a bit of glamour to a modern outdoor landscape. For fashion designer John Rocha's retreat on the French Riviera, opposite, a raised structure that keeps water flowing constantly over the edges creates a soft sculptural presence. Above left, a house in Morocco uses the small courtyard to full calming effect, with lounging space and a small reflecting pool, while in Bali, above middle, swimming and reflecting pools merge to form a circuit around the garden. Above right, water laps to the fine edge of a poured concrete patio.

Reflecting pools

02

In Los Angeles, opposite, a reflecting pool takes a visual leap through the glazed corridor of the house and beyond to the long lap pool. Below, swimming pools take on the character of the contemplative reflecting variety; left, sunset on a Florida inlet, with the light shimmering over man-made and natural bodies of water; right, a lap pool tucked beneath the wide, overhanging roof of a house in Rio de Janeiro is lit for the evening to a reflective glow.

Ponds

One step beyond the reflecting pool is the fish or lily pond, small pockets of naturally life-sustaining water. In the effortlessly exotic environs of Kuala Lumpur, below left, a house using very modern forms and materials offers the soothing experience of a simple koi pond. Below right, a grid of pond and gravel line the partly shaded walkway of a classic mid-century modern house by A. Quincy Jones in Southern California, while in New Zealand, opposite, the designers have taken a more natural approach, creating a rocky watering place planted with papyrus and surrounded with grasses and bright bedding plants.

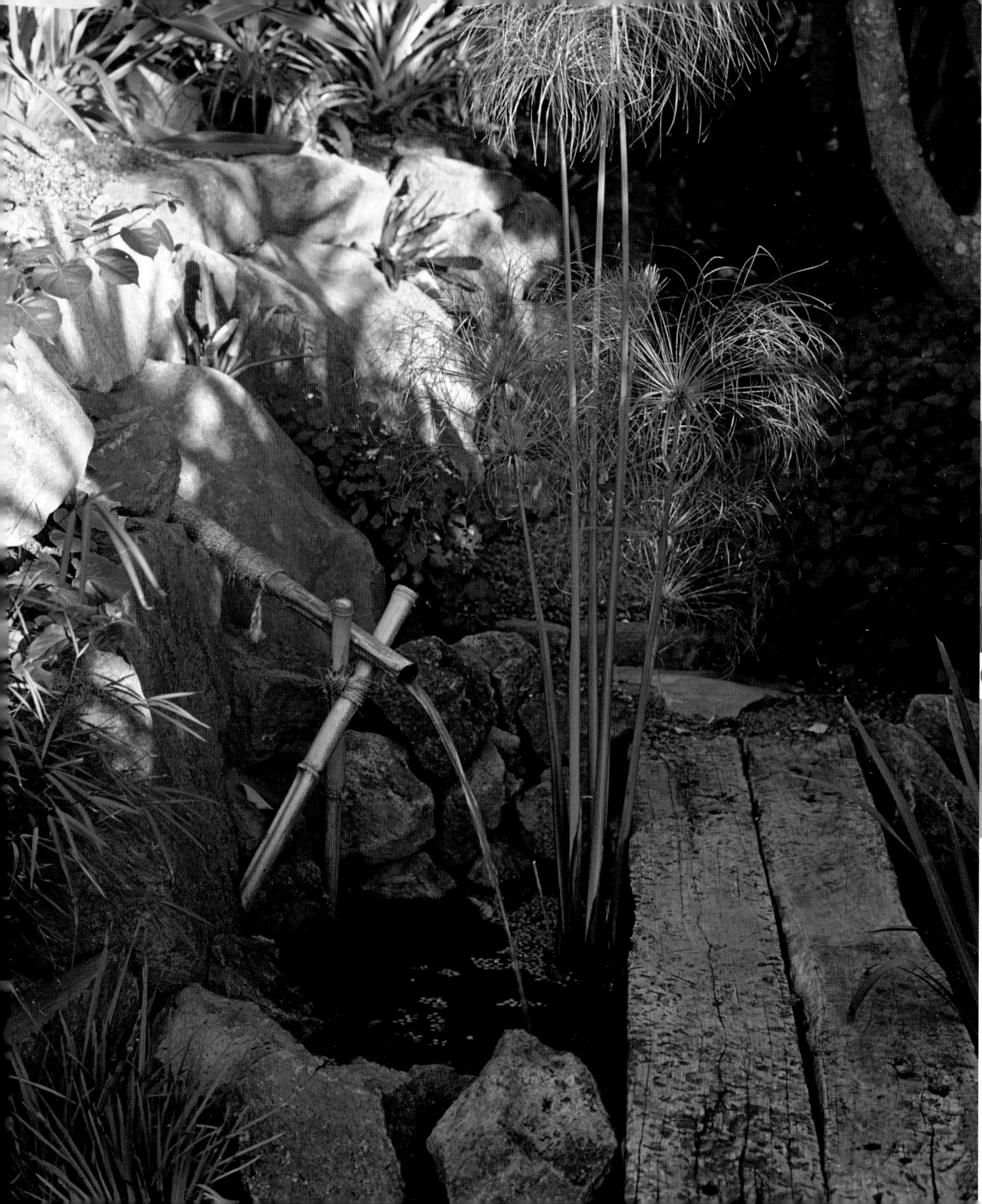

A timber-decked pathway to the swimming pool becomes a jungle catwalk in Bangkok, opposite. The pond, set beneath large-leaved banana trees on one side and the hanging greenery of the pergola and native plants beyond, has all the appearance of a natural body. Above left, an unabashedly modern insertion, the ovoid pool in this Singapore garden creates a dynamic geometry in the hard landscaping. Above, a bench floats above a lily pond in San Diego, where the blackened timber fence mimics the natural colour of the water. Above right, a man-made rock pond adds a bit of rustic appeal to the polished interior of a mid-century California house.

02

The dream of a tropical house is often about being on or near a natural body of water, whether on a sandy beach, at the edge of a sheltered inlet or a shimmering lake or by a meandering stream. A modern house and garden take their orientation from the position of the water, which some even incorporate into their design. Opposite and above left and middle, a house in Sri Lanka, built over land once used for cinnamon groves and later turned into a rubber plantation, retains the patchwork of paddy fields. Ancient trees were accommodated in the garden plan and statuary helps to define the boundaries. Above right, and following pages: another Sri Lankan house makes the existing rock and river part of the habitable structure.

Natural

02

02

Architecture

Indoor | outdoor
Hillside | levels
Open plan
Partitions

The building blocks of any house determine how well it can function as a domestic space or private retreat, and how well it fits into its surroundings and exploits the views. There are famous anecdotes of modern architects who, when asked how their design had been influenced by a particular site, proudly noted that they had not bothered to visit as their building would work in any situation. There are even more famous stories of how this turned out not to be true.

Nowadays, even the most devoted adherents of Modernism would pay some attention, respect even, to the terrain. Niemeyer and Bawa had distinctly different responses to the tropical landscape in their designs, but both are unquestionably 'of' the tropics – Bawa in his references to traditional building styles and attention to ventilation and light patterns, and Niemeyer in his somewhat outlandish forms that approximate the more spectacular botanical specimens of the rainforest. For the domestic architects in these pages, the questions of organization and form are more directly responsive to the environment.

The open-plan layout is especially advantageous in a warm climate, where the free circulation of air means the difference between an atmosphere that is comfortably salubrious and one that is unpleasantly stifling. It also lends itself to the indoor–outdoor flow of the tropical house, whether in the living room, perhaps covered with rugs or woven matting, or a patio/terrace. But an open-plan scheme usually calls for partitions of some kind, and many of the following designs incorporate carved or lattice screens, bringing the nuance of historical style and subtle patterns of light to play. Other, more modern partitions might be

more practical, to include storage, or made from interesting materials or in unusual forms to contribute texture and a sculptural presence.

With an indoor–outdoor scheme de rigueur in a tropical house, the way the interior follows naturally beyond the threshold is abetted by the open nature of modern architecture. Some architects have taken this to an extreme, not only through the use of a single, unifying floor surface, but also by extending the roofline beyond the walls of the house, even beyond where a traditional sheltered porch might be defined, while others have reinterpreted the courtyard, breaking

up the roof to create an open-air living space that is contained within the walls of the house, rather than at the edge.

But while an open plan on a single floor creates a free-flowing environment that can carry on easily to the outdoors, some tropical settings make the sprawling villa or bungalow impractical. And while a hilly terrain doesn't necessarily demand a multi-level house – think of all those bungalows perched on stilts, and indeed the Brazilian example here where the house is an orb elevated on slender legs – those levels can create a sense of

adventure, with surprising vistas and unusual spaces.

Some houses featured within these pages appear literally to be climbing a slope, with rooms set slightly above one another and stairs weaving between plants and rocks. In all of these cases, it is those decisions of form and style that imbue the structure with its basic attitude to its site, not providing a house suited to any place, but one suited to a specific place, and so making the most of what nature has provided as a starting point.

03

03

Indoor | outdoor

This is the lifestyle that most people come to the tropics for, one that moves easily from inside to the outdoors, from lounging in the living room to sipping drinks on the well-sited terrace. Previous pages: a classic modernist house by Craig Ellwood just north of Los Angeles opens the interior with a series of sliding doors and a patio surface that is level with the living room floor. A house in Australia, opposite, uses a change of material from the living room to the terrace, but maintains a level floor surface to encourage flow between the spaces. Above, three different modern designs in São Paulo offer unimpeded access to the open air, pool terrace and lush vegetation. A minimal interior scheme makes the transition even more natural.

03

Using materials on the interior that could also be applied to the exterior is one way of making a room feel totally versatile to outdoor living. Left, the grey tones and robust character of the formed concrete walls and marble flooring affirm the wide-open aspect of this house in Southern California. Open doors all around the structure let in natural sunlight, while the reflective surfaces of glass and polished marble bounce light through the sheltered space. Above, a house in the forest resort of Iporanga, near São Paulo, uses perforated metal sheets to function as both shutters and, when raised, shade canopies. The wooden floor extends to the outdoors, where it is left in a rougher condition for decking.

03

One of the characteristics of the modernist house that is well suited to the tropical climate is the low, wide overhanging roof, which creates a shaded perimeter that can be used for sheltered dining or lounging. Below left and opposite, a house in a tree-filled valley near Los Angeles makes full use of the extended roof to create a sheltered deck area. The extended cover makes it possible to use doors that swivel, rather than slide, to open up the room on two sides. Below right, a house in Singapore creates an indoor–outdoor effect with a double-height courtyard dining space. Retractable canvas awnings at roof level can be closed during heavy rain.

Hillside | levels

A house that is sited across different levels can seem a trying exercise to rationalize, but it can also present opportunities for bringing in light and for providing little areas of private retreat. Opposite, a house in New South Wales by Elizabeth Watson Brown features an upper-floor room that projects into the foliage. Below left, a house outside Los Angeles takes advantage of its elevated position to create a seating area with through-views to the palm-laden hillside. Below right, a modern house in Singapore features tactile materials interspersed with the natural hues and textures of the surrounding plants and trees. Following pages, the different levels in open-plan schemes all benefit from the free flow of light and ventilation.

03

Open plan

There is a lot to be said for open-plan living in a warm environment. While the absence of walls in a house in which heating is a priority would be challenging, the open plan in the tropics is a practical solution, as well as being attractive and flexible. Opposite, a Bawa-designed house in Sri Lanka has large rooms with expansive doorways that are well suited to an open-plan arrangement. Below, the iconic Sowden House in Los Angeles, by Lloyd Wright, son of Frank Lloyd Wright, is full of texture and pattern in the structural elements and provides a direct connection to the outdoor landscape. Following pages: a house near São Paulo functions like a modern, well-appointed pavilion, open inside and out.

03

03

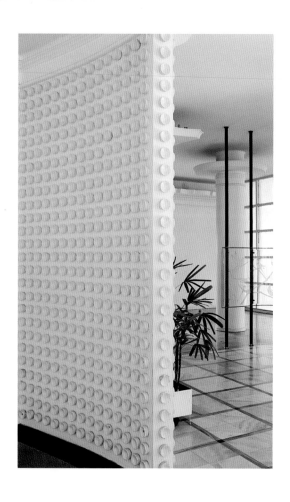

Partitions

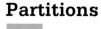

The fully open interior may not be to everyone's taste. But rather than create a warren of internal spaces, a clever way with partitions keeps light and air flowing, while screening particular areas of the floor plan. Above left, an apartment designed by Juan Pablo Rosenberg in a quirky 1950s block in São Paulo is divided by the cool curve of a textured partition. Above right, in an Australian house a clouded mirror separates the master bedroom and bath area. Opposite, more panels create a layering of light and privacy in another Brazilian house, where the clean, white interior is warmed up with natural wood flooring. Following pages: partitions as undulating enclosure (in a house designed by Greg Lynn of FORM), a storage wall, an elemental block divider, a partition with 'windows' in a Singapore apartment, and a display wall in a classic mid-century modern bungalow.

03

03

Elements

Stairs
Storage
Lighting
Windows | skylights
Doors | screens

It seems almost a shame to think of a tropical house in purely functional terms. One would rather concentrate on the view, the breeze, the sunset. But if a house is to be lived in, it has to cater as well as possible to more mundane needs. And since a feeling of ease is one of the most alluring aspects of life in warmer climes, the better integrated and the more practical elements are, the more attention can be given over to the satisfaction of aesthetic and atmospheric delights. And anyway, somehow it's a lot more fun to think about things like stairs, storage and windows when considering the

impact in a place that already has transcendent appeal.

The basic elements of structure and function that help to organize, illuminate and allow for movement through rooms and corridors become less conspicuous in the best designs for the modern tropical house. Unlike a house built in a traditional style, which will already have most of these choices predetermined, the new modern house will be planned to use every part to advantage and will exploit modern methods and materials to make those parts work efficiently. Some of these choices will no doubt be influenced by the

vernacular, which, after all, is a style that has developed in a particular region for good reason.

But in rethinking these styles, it is wise to consider how and why certain elements would be used in a particular way. For example, because sunlight is abundant in the tropics, it is sometimes taken for granted that there will be a lot of natural light coming into a house, and some necessary shade. But the placement of windows, the use of shutters or screens, the shape and size of these are all variations that have different effects and all are conscious choices in organizing a modern house to the

04

best and most comfortable effect. Similarly, stairs that perform the most basic task of getting people from one floor to the next can have a much larger impact on the interior, being open to allow natural light to filter down, or being staggered by split levels that create living spaces at half-intervals. These levels might all be open to view, not just through the interior, but also, with the help of large windows, in making the whole arrangement of levels visible from one elevation of the house through to the other, as if the entire internal geometry is part of the hillside and trees.

The incomparable quality of openness that a warm climate engenders is enhanced, of course, by open-plan spaces. But different regions also offer unique solutions to defining space, such as carved wood screens that exhibit traditional woodcraft and skill and can be given special prominence in a minimal interior. Doors that are carved, overlarge or made of special materials become a conspicuous design feature. And lighting that is attenuated for the darkest part of the evening also needs careful consideration, so as not to jar with a cool minimal or an updated colonial

theme. Some interiors in these pages take lighting design well beyond the realm of the practical, seeming to derive bold, colourful forms from the very flora of the jungle.

All of these elements can be implemented in very subtle ways as well, so that their design and function are almost invisible. That, too, is a conscious design decision, one that allows the tropical setting, and perhaps the more ornamental details, art and objects to have greater impact. The fun is in the mix, but the element of modern sophistication is, as ever, in the overall balance of parts.

Stairs

In tropical regions, an open stair encourages the flow of light and air, and makes the most of an interior geared to take in the beauty of the external surroundings. Opposite, a slimline metal staircase is left open along one side to make a minimal intrusion on the space. Below left, a 'floating' stair rises above an indoor pool in a cool, minimal interior. Below right, rough-hewn wood forms a more substantial stair for a house in São Paulo by Iodice Architects. Following pages: left, open stairs in open-plan spaces include zig-zag and freestanding circular forms, while open treads let even more light through the structure. On the right, swirling access to a spherical house designed by Eduardo Longo, also in São Paulo, defies the dictates of rectilinear design.

Lighting

It may seem that in equatorial climes all necessary light will flow naturally from the outside to bathe the interiors in glowing warmth. But artificial lighting has a place even in the sunniest of regions, and can form a shining contrast to more rustic elements, as in this traditional-style chandelier and candelabra for John Rocha's own retreat in France, above left and middle, or a Verner Panton-style lamp for a house in Los Angeles, above right. During the day the more sculptural presence of this distinctive ceiling light, opposite, by designer and architect Greg Lynn of FORM in Venice Beach, California, can be fully appreciated.

It is only fitting that this classic lamp adorns a house designed by Geoffrey Bawa in Sri Lanka, above left, as it too combines modern concepts with older patterns. Some lighting finds its best expression in forms that somehow mimic the extraordinary floral life of the tropics. Above right, a series of white ovoid pendants stand out against the irregular hues of variegated wood panelling in this Brazilian forest getaway. Opposite, the oversized pendant lamp has the shape and texture of an exotic fruit, but hangs in pure-white contrast against the thick forest greenery that marches to the edge of the terrace.

It is tempting to assume that storage is storage no matter where you live, but the high spaces and light of warm-weather houses and the open aspect of the interiors mean that storage is often a form of display, that items are not closeted away where the warm damp might reach them, but exposed to more light and air, albeit in an orderly fashion. A high wall of books is intriguing no matter where it appears, but light and space give the cultivated interior fresh appeal. On these pages, three modern California houses demonstrate the drama of books in bright spaces. Following pages: objects and articles, crockery, glass and utensils line open shelving, and display and storage cabinets are used for decorative effect and as room dividers.

Storage

Windows | skylights

Walls in a warm climate are all about windows: where, how large and what shape are all decisions that affect the light and warmth of the interior, and influence the degree to which the outdoors is allowed to be part of the experience of the living spaces. A hillside home in Rio de Janeiro, opposite, takes full advantage of its elevated position with massive windows opening to the surrounding trees. A house in Singapore, above left, and another in Sri Lanka, above middle, play on pattern and shape against textured surfaces; above right, an internal window provides an intriguing glimpse within Eduardo Longo's spherical house. Following pages: double-height windows, even those with paned glass, open living spaces to sky, sunlight and greenery, as do well-positioned and ample skylights. On the right, iconic designers Charles and Ray Eames made the most of the California sun with their double-height, fully glazed living room.

Doors | screens

Unlike in colder climates, where windows and doors need to provide a thermal barrier between the interior and the outdoors or between rooms, in tropical climes such solid separation is not so necessary, or indeed desirable. Though an entry door in Sri Lanka might be as solidly built as one in the Swiss Alps, it could also be larger and include perforated panels that allow a breeze to enter the house. And window shutters can also be more porous, providing shade, while at the same time letting in fresh air. Opposite, a Sri Lankan bedroom can be opened on two sides with decorative louvred doors. Right, a poolside patio is partially sheltered from sun and wind by a louvred wall. Following pages: doors and screens in varying degrees of transparency and decorative styling, ranging from the very modern to the traditional, all help temper sunlight, add a bit of privacy, and encourage all-important ventilation.

Light

Filtered
Dappled
Shaded
Pure
Layered | indirect
Soft

Light, along with water, is one of the most prized elements of the tropical zone. The warmth of the climate is one aspect, of course, but there is a measurable difference in the proximity of the sun when one is near the equator. Light is powerful in the tropics, so just having big windows and a gorgeous view will not do. Light must be filtered, directed, shaded, sculpted, even blocked in places to make living areas most comfortable. Like those in cold climates who face their gardens to the sun, the house in the tropics is orientated to take advantage of the natural warmth and light when

necessary, but also to protect the inhabitants from too much heat and glare.

Over the centuries, many cultures have developed architectural solutions to the problem of an overabundance of heat and light. The *mushrabiyah* in Islamic architecture, those delicately carved wooden screens, tame direct sunlight to softly patterned rays. Jalousie windows control ventilation, and can also be applied to modulate sunlight. The Venetian blind evolved from reed constructions used by the Egyptians through bamboo screens used in and around China. The idea with all of

these inventions was to let in some amount of light while discouraging thermal build-up. The placement of windows is another way in which the heat and glare of harsh sunlight can be modulated. Openings might be placed higher up a wall and made smaller, to avoid letting in large amounts of direct sun. Skylights might be baffled to redirect light, reducing glare and heat. Draperies, which have somehow lost their claim in the modernist sensibility, can now be manufactured from an array of high-tech fabrics that help to reduce heat while letting in light. There are even more thermally efficient fabrics

for keeping in heat in the evening, should that be a consideration.

And the orientation of rooms and the use of outdoor elements – pergolas, cloisters, courtyards – also help to modify or enhance heat and light in the tropical house. All of the age-old solutions have modern variations, the best ones taking advantage of tried and tested concepts to perform for a modern lifestyle. Screens can be deployed within the house, especially if the layout is open plan, to create degrees of softened light. And split levels, used perhaps to stack a series of rooms cleverly up an incline, can be

arranged with varying stages of exposure or shade. Even the natural foliage of a property, a giant palm or a forest canopy can be used wisely, with seating areas, walkways and terraces positioned in ways to take best advantage of the shady trajectory as the sun moves over the course of the day.

In this chapter, we've come up with some categories of light, descriptions that may seem quite fanciful – shaded, filtered, soft, pure, dappled, layered – but which address the real effects of sunlight as it is manipulated through the internal spaces. And though no one is

suggesting that design decisions are made to create some of these specific effects over others, it is worth observing how and in what situations such qualities of light are achieved. For some people, it is enough to feel the warmth of the tropical sunshine or to delight in the shimmering brilliance of low sun on a sparkling bay. But for those who want to make a modern life in the tropics, the possibilities for taming and focusing such a powerful natural resource can mean the difference between a house that shrinks from the sun and one that makes the most of its myriad powers.

Screens, shutters, shades and blinds, perforated panels or lattice-work window covers – in parts of the world where the heat of the midday sun is a force to be reckoned with, natural light needs some kind of mediating implement. Opposite, a small house in Los Angeles with long walls of glazing makes plentiful use of louvred screen and door panels for a muted effect indoors. Below left, a house in Sydney uses a wide-open window at one exposure and the tempering effect of blinds at the sunnier wall. Below right, criss-crossing shade across the deck of another California house is brought about by the pergola roof and palisade garden wall. Following pages: walls of glass bring softened light and provide privacy, while a clear end wall allows for a brighter experience for an indoor pool in a Brazilian house.

Filtered

05

Dappled

It may be one of life's more appealing accidental pleasures, but the dappled shade that comes from light through foliage is one of the most peaceful atmospheric gestures a space can have. Of added benefit are walls that are transparent enough to take in not only the view of the surrounding trees and plants, but also the effects of changing light and shade. Below, left to right, living room spaces in Sri Lanka, Brazil and Australia are enhanced by the natural patterns of sunlight. Opposite, in Los Angeles, a house designed with different internal levels set up within a largely transparent structure, benefits from the effects of natural light through varied heights and materials. Trees and outdoor planting are visible from many angles in the living space, and an elevated seating area takes indirect sun from a skylight positioned to act as a visual room divider.

05

Moving through the cool shadows and shifting
patterns of naturally tempered sunlight is a softly
serene experience. Opposite, a house designed
by California modernist Ray Kappe is an essay in
natural lighting effects. The open-plan interior is
cleverly arranged to suggest a perimeter walkway
between living areas that takes in the light and
shade of the garden. Below, an Australian house
with a narrow side yard makes maximum use of an
opportunity to open a great window and use the
natural shading effects of the overgrowing trees.

Shaded

We may crave the sun, but we also need a break from it at times. A livable house allows for both conditions. In places where sunshine is abundant, a shady retreat or a darkened, cool corner is a calming space. Opposite, a bungalow in New Zealand alternates large glass walls with solid structure to form spaces that are exposed or sheltered from light. Right, the curving planes of this avant-garde California house affect the view and the reach of natural light into the interior. Following pages: left, the undulating roof of an experimental house in Australia creates a softly scalloped clerestory, while elsewhere an extended roof overhang creates shade both inside and out. In other places, a woven screen and overgrown window trellis keep interiors cool. Right, a Brazilian house with generous glazing on the ground floor uses a block of stairs to help shade a lower-floor area.

And then there is the thrill of pure, poured sunlight, the kind that when you are viewing it from a cold, damp place, you feel you want to absorb. It is the light that goes along with white walls and fabrics, as in this minimalist house in São Paulo, opposite, whose giant glass doors freely admit pure, untempered sun. Below, left to right, a skylight breaks the shell of a California house, bathing the dining room in sun; a skylit bathroom is a revelation as approached from the confines of the darkened hallway; and Eduardo Longo's sphere house in the heart of São Paulo is a contained oasis of pure forms and light.

Pure

05

Some of the most intriguing effects can be
achieved when light, whether natural or
artificial, arrives in layers or by indirect means.
This can be a result of the different structural
levels within the house, varied window
positions, or by partitions that are used instead
of solid walls so that light is allowed to flow into
a space from different points in the house.
Below left, both large glass walls and internal
walls topped with a glazed clerestory let light
run through the space from several angles.
Below right, doors, windows and skylights all
let in sunlight, but with wonderful variations
in position and intensity. Opposite, a narrow,
horizontal window opening is a good way to let
in light and maintain some privacy, especially
when there are other light sources available.

Layered | indirect

Shade can be as layered as light, as the daring concrete house in Brazil, left, belonging to artist Tomie Ohtake demonstrates. The glazed end wall creates brightly lit perimeter spaces, while the elegantly angled concrete planes give dynamism to the low-slung interior. Above, a hallway becomes a journey of light and dark in this California house, where a transparent threshold leads visitors from the darkened corridor through a box of light, before presenting the main living space.

With artificial light we might make use of a dimmer switch or a frosted bulb to achieve an effect that is both soothing and inspiring; with an interior that is designed to take in natural light, the condition is achieved through a combination of exposing and shading a room to direct sunlight. Opposite, large windows do not have to mean being overexposed to sun, as the further rooms are tucked into the core of the house, the less light they will feel. One benefit of an open-plan environment is that furnishings can be moved to areas of greater or lesser degrees of shade. The use of wood on the floor and ceiling also softens the effect of the sun. Below, more dining areas set just inside the reach of the sun's rays are warm without being too bright.

Soft

Materials matter when screening out sunlight. Above, left to right, in this bathroom space a wall of glass blocks brings a generous amount of light into the room, while softening its effect and providing privacy; a cathedral ceiling leaves enormous space for light and air with windows at either end and a polished concrete floor making a gently reflective surface; and an unusually shaped window opening makes for a bright corner office space and a more tempered light in the main living area. Opposite, the grand sweep of this arcing window wall in Brazil could easily overwhelm a space with harsh sunlight, but judiciously placed opposite the lush hillside, it becomes a frame for a salubrious portion of light and landscape.

Function

06

Living
Lounging
Cooking | eating
Entertaining
Work
Bathing
Sleeping

Every house must have its functional spaces – even a glorious holiday home should be able to cater to the basic activities of eating, sleeping and relaxing. But then there is also the possibility of entertaining guests to stay, or just for an afternoon poolside barbecue. And though it may seem anathema to the tropical setting, there are those who will want to do some kind of work from home, whether theirs is a holiday retreat or a year-round dwelling that happens to be in an equatorial region. This is what differentiates the tropical modern home from the glorified vacation hut – it is a house that possesses the spaces and flexibility for full-time living.

Of course, being functional doesn't preclude a house from also being modern, stylish or eclectic, just as being modern doesn't discount ideas of comfort or originality. The really exciting houses and interiors are those that are able to fulfil the demands of modern living while maintaining their inherent tropical appeal, whether in decoration or design. Modern living spaces increasingly favour an open-plan, flexible arrangement of interior spaces, and this is especially true in warm climates where the free circulation of air is crucial to the pleasant atmosphere of the house. In addition to being open between different functional areas, the tropical house will be open to the elements, with floor-to-ceiling windows or large, sliding doors to emphasize the indoor–outdoor lifestyle that is such an important part of tropical living.

So living spaces will be open, and the area for cooking and eating will likely also be visible from the main living space, or segregated by multi-use partitions, such as bookcases or shelving, or by a decorative screen. But this openness, as important as it may be for ventilation and the ease of

movement, does not mean that private areas cannot be cleverly separated and given their own particular ambience. Bedrooms and bathrooms also have a distinctive character in warmer climates, with greater need for ventilation and the ability to be open to lots of warm sunlight or shaded from intense heat or for privacy. Here, too, larger windows create a liberating welcome to the outdoors, while outdoor planting can become part of the overall decor. And since open showers and bath areas are more common, trying to enclose heated rooms is not usually an issue.

Outdoor spaces can be left in casual arrangements for lounging on the poolside or terrace, or set out with more fixed order for al fresco entertainment. Either way, the key is to take advantage of areas where shade can be utilized, under an overhanging roof, for instance, or beneath mature trees, and ideally within easy reach of the kitchen and indoor eating areas.

And while it might seem like the last thing you would want to do in a beautiful modern house in an exotic location, the idea that some sort of work at home might be necessary is not only a possibility, for some people

it is the quiet tropical seclusion that most inspires productivity. So areas for work often need to be part of the scheme. But these spaces need not be relegated to a closed-off basement, so that work is made to feel like more of a punishment. The work space, too, should be provided with plenty of light and air, so that work is more like another aspect of living that becomes tinged with the feeling of ease and positive thinking that the presence of so much natural beauty and sun is able to bestow.

A living space is the centre of most homes –
despite the appeal of gathering in the kitchen –
and is the room that needs to be the most
flexible. The open-plan living scheme is
particularly suited to houses in warm climates
where the overlarge doors or windows can be
opened to encourage the flow of fresh air.
Opposite, the Skywave house in California
by Anthony Coscia includes a living area
suspended in a free-floating mezzanine. The
house was meant to combine the flexibility
of an artist's studio with an indoor–outdoor
fluidity. Below left, a floor-to-ceiling window is a
dramatic backdrop in an elevated living space.
Below right, white walls make for a bright
interior in this bungalow outside of Sydney.

Living

Opposite, a house in Singapore designed by
WOHA Architects features rich teak flooring and
sliding doors that have the delicate gauzy effect
of Japanese shoji screens. The small reflecting
pool set just beyond the roofline adds to the
peaceful atmosphere of the room. Above, left to
right, the living room opens to an inner
courtyard in São Paulo, with the brick of the
external wall bringing a sense of the outdoors
to the interior space; bold spots of colour are
used against a neutral palette in this open-plan
sitting room in Rio de Janeiro, where the jungle
vegetation makes a lush background; and
industrial materials – steel and concrete –
are softened with overflowing plants and
natural light.

Less focused than even the most versatile living space, a place for lounging is one that is all about relaxation. These are the most tranquil of the public areas of the house, and anticipate those moments of rest or inspiration that feel pleasantly unplanned. Below, left to right, a rattan chaise longue is well suited to the traditional timber window fittings and weighty stone terrace of this Sri Lankan house; a California house displays a more modern approach to rattan furnishings, with sharp, circular pieces set on a stone-paved terrace; and an enclosed terrace in Sydney provides shade from harsh summer sun with a generous pergola. Opposite, fashion designer John Rocha has created a zen-like atmosphere in his garden on the French Riviera with seamless paving and an array of seat cushions that can be gathered up or rearranged with ease. Following pages: some of the most enchanting seating areas are those in secreted outdoor spaces.

Lounging

Cooking | eating

These are essential spaces, where the vital activities of preparing food, cooking and eating happen, but they are also social areas. In places where temperatures and humidity soar, kitchens need ample ventilation. High ceilings and lots of large windows make kitchen areas appealing places to gather, even in warm weather. Left, the kitchen in Anthony Coscia's Skywave house is just another 'area' housed within the open, double-height shell. Glass doors on either side provide the kitchen with plenty of natural light and fresh air. Opposite, the kitchen of this low-profile California house is bordered by a long, low window opening and an outdoor pond. Following pages: more kitchen and dining areas, characterized by high ceilings and expansive windows.

For some, the best part of having a beautiful house is being able to share it. The tropical habits of living between indoors and out, of open spaces and light are all conducive to entertaining. Opposite, the forest resort of Iporanga, Brazil, has many attractions. Below left, poolside dining is casually elegant with mature palms swaying above a white-washed garden wall. Below right, this very modern house can adapt to changes in weather and lifestyle and accommodate indoor dining and al fresco meals with ease. Following pages: modern dining spaces filled with natural light and splashes of inspired eclecticism.

Entertaining

The best work spaces are clean, stylish and comfortable, no matter where they are located. Below left, a smart Brazilian apartment contains a small but flexible office space. The materials – unfinished concrete, blond wood and glass blocks – all recall various periods of Modernism. Below right, white walls and floor, which might otherwise be glaring for a main living space, are enlivening in an artist's studio in São Paulo that is awash with sunlight. Opposite, an elegant modern house in the Brazilian jungle, with spaces that flow freely between the interiors and the outdoors, accommodates a work area with easy, though possibly distracting, access to the poolside deck.

Work

Bathing

Water is an elemental attraction of the tropics. So when water comes indoors, the inclination is to make it feel a natural part of the experience of the house. Though privacy is obviously a priority, bathing spaces in the tropical dwelling can be much more open to natural sunlight and fresh air, with inventive modern methods of seclusion. Opposite, a California house designed by Greg Lynn makes use of his trademark curvaceous forms, with a bowl-shaped, freestanding bath and continuous tiling. Above, left to right, a vivid purple curtain offers a veil of privacy in an otherwise open bathing space; Lloyd Wright's designs for the Sowden house in California are all about texture and pattern, with a small courtyard providing a further sense of luxury; and the peaceful, spare decor of this austere bathroom is the very essence of elegant minimalism.

For some reason, a warmer climate provides the freedom to experiment with daily rituals, whether it is going back to basic ways of cleansing or embracing the outdoor experience. Below left, a house in California juxtaposes basic materials – glass and concrete – in discreet modern planes. Below right, a cutting-edge flat in São Paulo contains a shower that poses a quirky new take on a very old-fashioned bathing concept. Opposite, a house in Sydney features a bath dropped into the floor; when covered with teak panels, it forms a continuous surface that becomes an external walkway. Uncovered, the bath sits in cool harmony with the bordering pond and giant ferns.

Innovative window designs, a carefully chosen palette of materials and clever screening are all factors in creating a comfortable, well-ventilated sleeping area. Opposite, Ray Kappe's iconic modernist house in the Los Angeles hills has an open sleeping space with sunlight streaming in through large windows and a clerestory above. The generous use of natural wood provides a warm contrast to the rough concrete and glass. Above left, a pair of old lift doors has been repurposed as a headboard and screen divider. A curtain can be drawn to block the view through the delicate, wrought-iron filigree panels. Above middle, another elegant Australian sleeping area features a narrow, vertical window with glass louvres to allow for ventilation, as well as a large side window that opens the room to the forest. Above right, an external timber screen closes off a guest bedroom to the view and sun, but not the cooling breeze.

Sleeping

Taking advantage of the screening possibilities
of the surrounding native vegetation is one way
to create private spaces that are luxuriously free
of physical boundaries. Above, a holiday home
near Kuala Lumpur features a pavilion-like
sleeping space in a room lined with fully
opening window panels. With its sparse
furnishings and encroaching forest, the room
has the charmed atmosphere of a tree house.
Traditional lightweight hammocks replace
bulky bed-and-mattress combinations.
Opposite, the myriad trees and plants that
surround this house in Bangkok bely its urban
setting. The voluminous vegetation creates an
effective privacy zone around the glass-walled
living and sleeping areas.

Furniture

Bright
Modern
Exotic
Outdoor
Wood
Built-in

When the shipwrecked Robinson Crusoe began work on his 'habitation', the first items of furniture that he made for himself were a table and a chair. It is not clear what materials he used, probably wood he had recycled from the foundered ship or scavenged from the island, but he does make a point of saying that he remade both pieces until he was satisfied with their design. The modern tropical house wants furniture that conveys a sense of modern style, but that also somehow reflects the luxuriant environs. In any case, there ought to be a discernible coherence or logic to

furniture choices. This is not to make a show of great effort in design, but rather to sustain the feeling of ease by keeping any awkward juxtapositions to a minimum. Even Robinson Crusoe wanted things to function properly and to his liking.

When one utters the word 'tropical', many people will eagerly envision bright and bold patterns and colours that reflect the most vivid equatorial hues. And those certainly come to the fore in these pages, as part of a tropical decor that is charming and enlivened by those deep tones. In a similar vein, one

might choose furnishings that exhibit the exoticism of the region. Traditionally styled pieces in carved wood or woven tapestries make a connection to local vernacular, and yet also, in the modern house, reveal a fresh sense of style. Then there are other objects made from wood that may not express a local character, but by their solidity and native material make their own connection with the natural setting.

But as we're talking here about houses that are both 'tropical' and 'modern', there is also room for furniture that is more unabashedly of the latter persuasion – furniture that

is stylish, minimal, subtle and sophisticated. Just as the low-lying, glass-walled bungalow of the International Style seemed to blossom as a cool modern icon when transplanted to warmer regions, modernist-style furnishings take their place as rational objects in the verdant landscape, perhaps becoming even more sculptural and profound when considered against the natural profusion of a jungle setting. Before the furnishings are added in, if the design has been very forward-thinking and the ease of living truly a component, then some kind of built-in furniture will be part

of the scheme, in keeping with the style of the house and to minimize the need for superfluous 'stuff'. Piles of books may suit a nineteenth-century library in northern Europe, but the warm, humid climate of the tropics wants cleaner surfaces, and less accumulation.

The same applies to the outdoors, where there will be abundant opportunities to insert a civilized place for sitting, eating, drinking, relaxing. Among the hibiscus and the fern, beneath the palm, the mango or the orchid tree, a table and chair, a lounger, a bench. They can be built into a hillside or deck, or be

movable pieces that allow for more flexibility and let the lounger follow the sun or shade with a book, a pillow, or a Mai Tai, but outdoor furnishings are more an integral part of the lifestyle of the tropical house than any in colder climates. If living outdoors is part of the attraction, then furnishing the outdoors is a priority of design and comfort.

The exotic sometimes needs nothing to compete with it. On the other hand, the jungle might just inspire some wilder choices. Furnishings should function, but they should also inspire a bit of joy. Even strong sunlight can't wash out this bubble-gum pink dining table, opposite, which combines cool minimal form with high-spirited colour. Below left, further subtle spots of colour lift an otherwise neutral palette in little exclamations of surprise. Below right, an Eames 'Tulip' chair has been covered in a modernist-style pattern of bold stripes. It is the perfect injection of colour in a smart Brazilian apartment.

Bright

07

More fun with colour. Artist Jean-François Fourtou's house in Morocco, below left, is filled with bold, soft furnishings that mix curving, organic shapes with exuberant hues. The white walls and natural light keep the more vivid parts anchored in the scheme. Below right, an ornate upholstered side chair is paired with a crystal chandelier in the skylit shower area of a modern California house, setting up all sorts of contrasts between modern and traditional, light and colour, hard and soft surfaces. Opposite, the cushions of this outdoor divan, covered in a fabric designed by the owner, demonstrate how a stroke of radiant colour brings a neutral palette and more subtle textures to life.

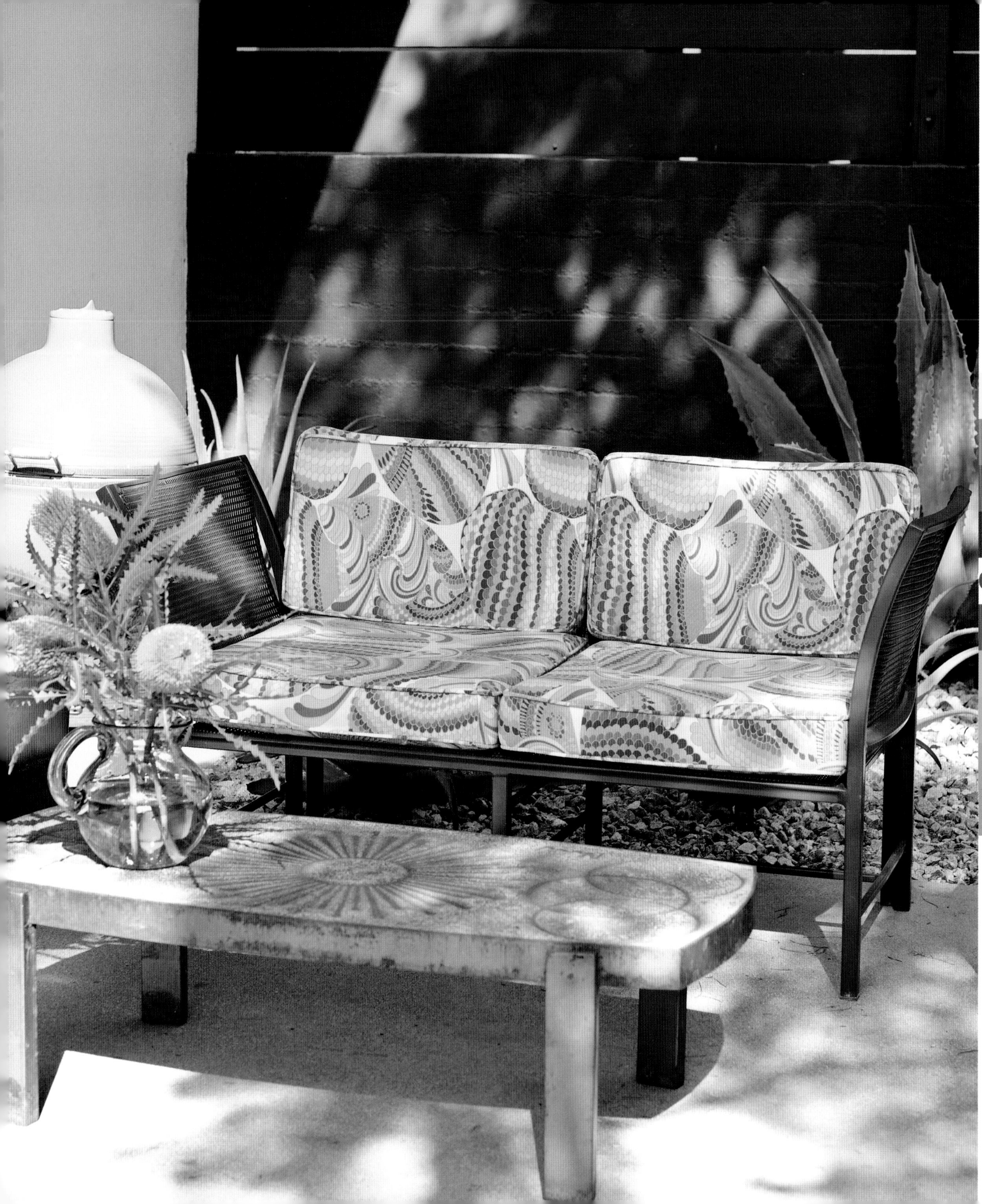

Modern

Modern icons, like good modern architecture, have a place in any sophisticated design scheme. Opposite, a 1960s 'Seagull' chair, manufactured by Fritz Hansen, invites a bit of lounging in the light-filled living room of a Los Angeles antiques dealer. Below right, in the same house, designed by California modernist A. Quincy Jones, the patio was enclosed to create another bright living area with a Hans J. Wegner-designed 'Papa Bear' chair. Below left, another iconic chair design, 'La Chaise' by Charles and Ray Eames, contributes to the elegant minimalism of a Singapore interior. Following pages: left, modern furniture highlights in the context of California, Brazil and New Zealand; right, architect and designer Greg Lynn produced his own style of modern utility in his California house.

Exotic

Part of the allure of living in the tropics is being able to embrace the exotic, the native patterns, textures and materials that have grown out of the lush natural environment. Set within a clean, modern context, the intricate craftsmanship and design of a delicate wood screen or carved chair back is allowed to stand out. Opposite, in Sri Lanka a bed made of decorative carved wood panels, dressed with simple, starched linens, offers a cool place for repose. Right, a pool terrace in Colombo features an intriguing colonial-style settee, which becomes a focal point on the unadorned concrete patio against the vines and palms beyond.

07

The appeal of the exotic lies in the conjuring of faraway places. Above left, a modernist house in the hills near Los Angeles was restored to its original open style by its owners, who are antiques dealers. The burled wood drawers give the impression of a stack of cases ready for a long adventure. Above middle, interior designer Tony Duquette was known to eschew any sense of restraint in favour of the lavish, even the outlandish, to give his home an atmosphere of thoughtful extravagance. The Oriental-style cabinet is one of a host of ornate pieces that envelop the interior in a world of exotic fantasy. Above right, a carved-wood settee, and opposite, a vintage colonial-style daybed invite a moment of relaxation in two Sri Lankan homes.

07

Outdoor

Outdoor furnishings in the tropics are much more than a pleasant afterthought. These are spaces that can be inhabited year round and for nearly all activities, so tables and seating are often a mix of hardy modern and rustic. Opposite, a pair of sculptural lounge chairs in a Brazilian garden. Above left, a solid plank of naturally veined wood provides generous space for outdoor dining in Morocco. Above right, a classic piece of modern design by Eero Aarnio hangs amid the ferns in a California backyard setting. Following pages: left, open-area seating in Morocco, California, Sri Lanka and Sydney; right, a bench of tubular metal rods provides a pathway rest area in the garden of a house by Oscar Niemeyer, outside Los Angeles.

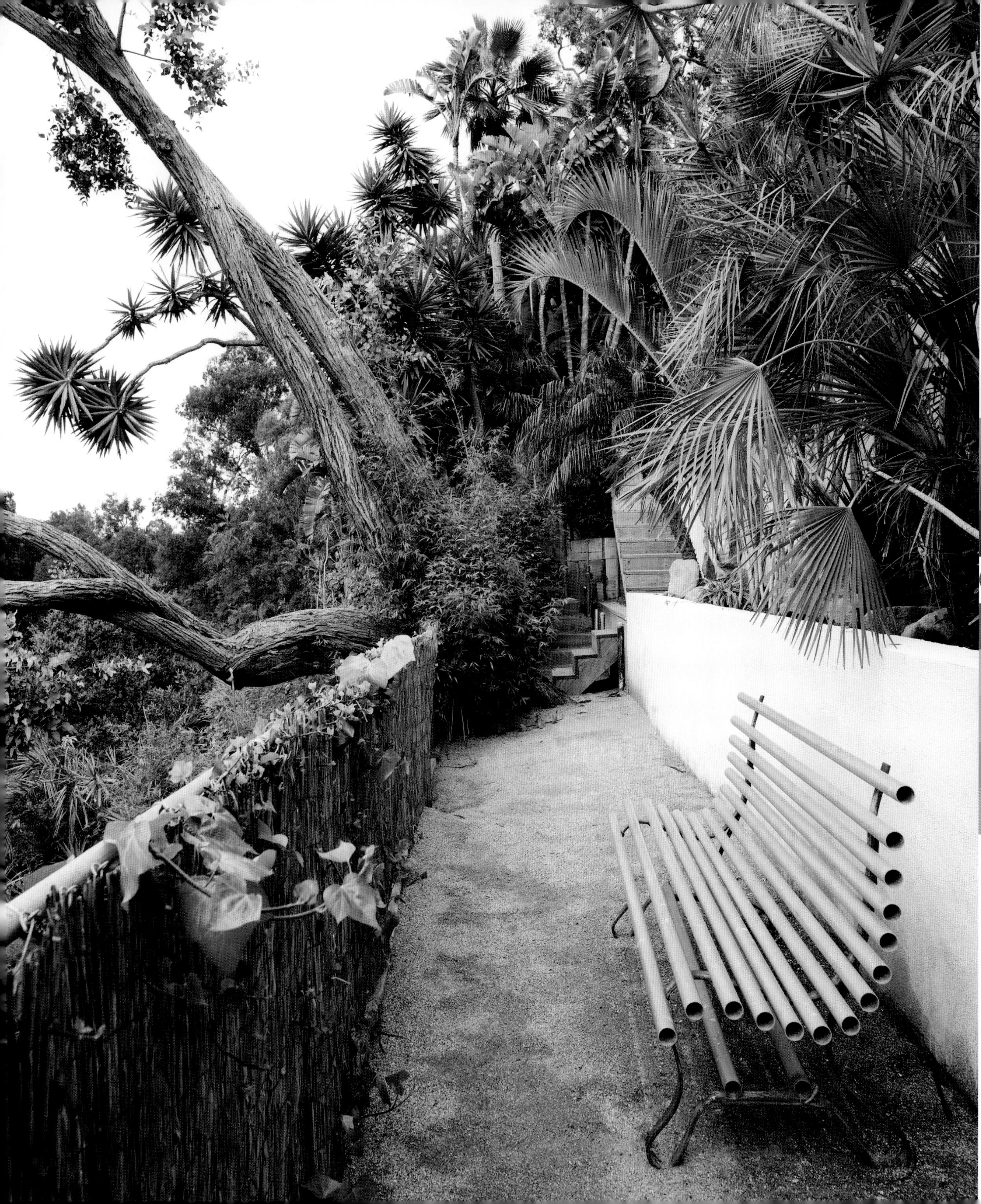

Furnishing outdoor spaces well has a lot to do with view and position. Left, the owners of an iconic house designed by Oscar Niemeyer took advantage of its position on a hillside ridge by making a series of terraced seating areas, which are idyllic spots for taking in the view of the local mountains and valley. Below, in the forested area around São Paulo, a modern house in concrete and glass offers an array of 'civilized' outdoor spaces, including this pool deck with hardwood recliners.

07

Wood

Wood is the most elemental of furniture materials and has a particular appeal in the open environment of a warm-weather climate, where giant forests present an array of exotic species with varying hues and textures. Below left, a bentwood stool is both distinctively modern and natural. Below right, a pair of low-slung armchairs made from dark tropical wood maintains the modernist rustic ambience of a Brazilian forest retreat. Opposite, a wooden pedestal chair in the bath area of this Los Angeles house is part of a tropical vignette, created with the help of the palm-frond wall covering.

07

 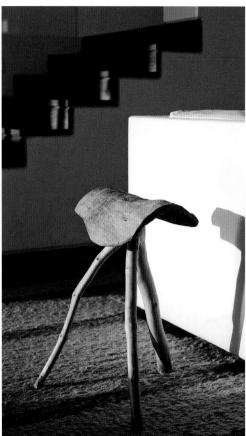 

The irregular pattern and colour of natural wood
makes a nice contrast with the clean lines of
the cool palette of a modern interior. Above left,
a pair of antique carved chairs in a traditional-
style house with modern arrangements in
Sri Lanka. Above middle, a rustic seat of
unfinished wood in Brazil, and above right, the
material in a highly polished and sophisticated
three-legged design by Hans J. Wegner is part
of a modern Australian interior. Opposite, the
classic modern forms of Mies van der Rohe
dining chairs highlight the hardy endurance of
a solid acacia wood table top that retains its
natural imperfections.

07

If being in the tropics is about a certain ease of living, then the modern concept of creating furniture that is part of the internal structure of the house is one to be celebrated. When the desire is for a natural flow of light, air and people from one space to another, then it helps to have minimal intrusions of large furnishings. The smooth flow of form and colour is key to the bright and easy-going atmosphere in this house by Greg Lynn, opposite, and in the lipstick-red bath, below middle, designed by architect Hugh Buhrich for a home on the outskirts of Sydney. Below left, the integration of sofa, stair and bookcase maximizes utility and minimizes the furnishing footprint. Below right, underneath a run of windows in a corner of the dining area is the perfect place to tuck away bench seating. The low position of the windows gives diners a clear view of outdoor greenery.

Built-in

07

Bold
White
Natural
Pattern
Art | objects
Texture
Fabrics

When asked to conjure up the colours of the tropics, many people will imagine something from Gauguin's paintings of French Polynesia: the forthright figures and bold strokes of vivid hues. There is nothing subtle in the light or the palette. For Gauguin, painting for a European audience, it was as if he needed to convey every colour and perhaps every sensation (the bursting of ripe fruit, for example) in one composition. But for the modern visitor, it is the wide expanses of blue sky, green forest, white beach that are most alluring. Those more ebullient colours exist, but in the context of the larger, undisturbed natural setting, they are rarer delights.

As with any house in any context, there are many ways to express a theme or personality in the tropics, and to highlight the cultural context or physical surroundings. Here, we consider several types of decorative details that, while applicable to most houses, work in certain ways in the tropical setting. Colour is an important factor in tropical design, of course, as there may be competing hues from the natural world – even a blazing sunset can be made to look different through the prism of a spare or abundant interior. We look at the use of a white backdrop, which in some cases provides a brilliant contrast to more colourful accents, but in others, like a space age-style interior in Brazil, the white living 'zone' becomes a holistic retreat from both the built-up and the verdant environments.

Natural background tones can also be employed to provide a contrast, but tend to create more of a comforting blend of objects and colours. While traditional methods and building materials make sense in any region, the promise of the pure modernist, white-washed form offers

08

an opportunity for highlighting the brighter natural background and details. So the exterior treatment of the house becomes part of the stylistic consideration, especially when there are lots of outdoor spaces, or 'rooms', from which the form and colour of the architecture will be on display.

For houses that function as indoor–outdoor living spaces, a change in textural detail, whether on the floors or walls, in wood screens or shutters, provides definition and variation to spaces, especially where fabric furnishings might be scarce due to warm weather – although

fabrics, from gauzy draperies to ethnic weavings, also make for a bit of drama and richness, even when used sparingly. And while the idea of the modern tropical house might suggest a spare shelter that takes its decorative animation from the fecund surroundings, as in any home, the atmosphere is charged with the aesthetic inspiration of carefully chosen art and objects, whether they reflect a high personal taste or pay homage to the lush, sun-drenched location.

The house may not resemble the profusion of Gauguin, but a refined collection of details that brings

'tropical' and 'modern' into a more complementary relationship. It may be that a landscape of brilliant greenery and vivid flora inspires you to emulate a similarly striking palette indoors. The most pleasing combinations will allow the well-chosen flashes of inspiration to stand out among a more subdued background, unless, of course, the whole is one big flash of brilliance, as with some examples here. But the more prevailing choices are those that allow a peaceful semblance of harmony between the most enticing tropical elements and thoughtful modern principles.

Bold

'Bold' is a term that seems made for the equatorial island climate. With so much clear sunlight about, it seems only natural to want to spread more colour around, whether in large portions or in a profusion of blooming details. Below left, a neutral background takes on vivid accents in a modern Brazilian interior. Below right, in the double-height main space of a Sri Lankan house, a few bright details boost a spare arrangement. Opposite, in this house in Los Angeles by Barbara Bestor, the internal living space is divided by a barn-style door, painted in deep red. Following pages: more crimson devotions in the Brazilian 'red sphere' house by Lucas Longo, and in interiors from Los Angeles to Morocco.

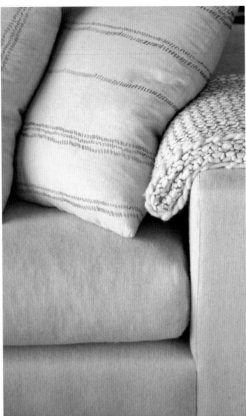

White

For some, modernism is all about white, the purity of colour to match that of singular form. But there are many shades and textures that make white more than just a background hue. Above, left to right, a clean, white interior frames a verdant view in Morocco; layers and textures add richness to a white interior; and the complementary combination of white fabrics against dark, tropical wood is a perennial classic. Opposite, in a Brazilian house, surrounded by the many bold colours and textures of the jungle, white walls and fabrics create a cool, peaceful haven.

08

The Complete Earth

Natural

What better way to express an appreciation of the natural environment than to incorporate natural tones, textures and materials into the interior scheme. Opposite, with fully opening window walls, the interior of this Brazilian house stretches beyond the 'internal' spaces with natural wood flooring that extends to decking of a similar tone. The subtle colourway of the floor rug chimes with the honeyed brick walls and leather furnishings. Below left, the house of legendary German expatriate architect Hugh Buhrich, near Sydney, uses natural wood in an array of layers and patterns. Below right, this Bali retreat creates a series of calm spaces with modern and antique wood elements, along with light fabrics.

Pattern

Pattern in nature is one of the more intriguing areas of biology. Intricate expressions of symmetry are everywhere. It is only natural that pattern should pervade a nature-loving interior, as in this airy Brazilian house, opposite, and the more fulsome arrangement of texture and colour in Los Angeles, left. Following pages: left, a mid-century apartment building in São Paulo is part Art Deco, part brightly coloured fantasy, and happily saved from demolition. The white-painted iron grille creates a decorative flourish against the dark-pink wall, which contrasts with the more subdued modernism of the apartment interior. Right: patterns in wood, metal, tiles and textiles are used as screening devices, wall ornaments and sculptural additions.

08

Art | objects

The things that make a home are those that have a real connection to the people who live there. Even an expression of high Modernism is personalized by the owner who is an absolute devotee, and not just following a trend. At the other end of the spectrum are those who collect and want to show off their accumulated treasures. Today 'modern' is about that compromise between sensible minimalism and self-expression. Opposite, the Moroccan home of artist Jean-François Fourtou is the setting for a playful menagerie of sculptural creatures. For artist Tomie Ohtake in Brazil, above left, and designer Greg Lynn in Los Angeles, above middle, art is a part of the interiors. Above right, in a cool Brazilian interior, even a bit of well-known trademarking can have its artful impact. Following pages: more art in the tropics from Fourtou, left, and elsewhere in Sri Lanka, Morocco and São Paulo.

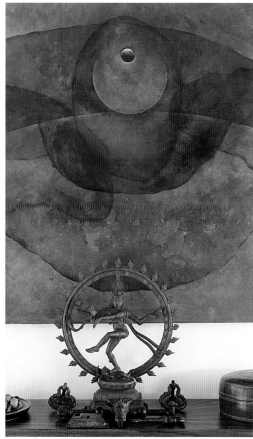
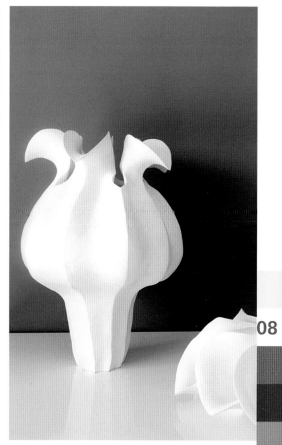

08

The tropics are all about texture, of bark and foliage, running water and still pools, with interiors also inspired by a texture of natural, untreated materials. Opposite, a mosaic wall in a modern California house adds richness to an otherwise spare living space, and contrasts with the smooth forms of the concrete floor and leather sofas. Below left, in Sydney a dramatic bathing experience was created with an oversized bath built into the floor space, and tiled in dark, irregular pieces that reflect the stone's natural imperfections. Below right, a bamboo curtain makes a light-filtering room divider in a Singapore apartment. Following pages: the intriguing surface textures of stone, metal and brick and, in California, an undulating carpet of bog grass.

Texture

Fabrics

Sheer, lightweight and often whimsical, fabrics used in tropical interiors convey the easy style of warm-weather living. Where more solid solutions are unnecessary, fabric can be used to filter direct sunlight, to add a bit of pattern or colour, or to separate a corner or room. Opposite, a traditional-style cotton fabric covers a low bed in a contemporary modern house in Morocco. Above left, in a large Sri Lankan house, layers of fabrics hung casually across a wall infuse the room with local colour, texture and patterns. In fashion designer John Rocha's retreat on the French Riviera, above middle, the cool minimal palette is embellished with ethnic weavings in neutral tones, while in another sunny French interior, above right, soft curtains cast a soothing shade of pink over a sunken bath.

Wood
Tiles
Stone
Glass
Brick
Concrete
Metal
Mixed-media

In the tropics, there is an immediacy in our experience of nature. This is not an alpine location, where the rock face stares back at you from a distance, or a desert, where the scrub vegetation spreads out into an arid horizon. Here, the leaves and branches, the river, lake and sea are close by in the moisture-hung atmosphere. The scent of burgeoning flora is haunting, pervasive; the texture of the plants and trees, even pools of water, are in visible relief. Our appreciation of each material's inherent properties is intensified.

The use of wood is taken for granted in the tropics, from carved objects to natural, untreated grain. One type of wood relates to another, and offers a continuum with the forest beyond. But wood is not always a rustic pillar or plank. Smooth, highly polished hardwood has a more modern effect than rough-hewn logs, but both can be part of a modern house that engages with the landscape. Other materials, such as stone, are also part of the evolution of tropical architecture. Think of the temple of Angkor Wat in Cambodia, its thistle-shaped towers surrounded by a tangle of jungle greenery, or the ruins of some other ancient stone shrine, wrapped in centuries of creeping verdure, old stone as a part of a new dwelling, or newly chiselled segments that offer an intrinsic connection to the landscape.

There are other designers who seem to defy the natural tendencies of materials in these locations, and choose something outside of the local realm, emphasizing perhaps the fact that the building is already an intrusion. Concrete has long been used in tropical climates for unmistakably modern forms that sit in clear distinction from their surroundings, useful especially for nonlinear forms, being more curved

or rounded like shapes in nature. Oscar Niemeyer's famous Catedral de Brasília is a stunning example of how pure forms of concrete can be used to express exoticism and contrast with abundant vegetation.

Glass, once a luxury for reasons of cost and thermal efficiency, is now available in different specifications that can help to reduce solar gain tremendously. And the potential for opening up the interior with glass is seemingly unlimited: a long window-wall stretching beneath a wide, overhanging roof gives a protected view, while introducing indirect sunlight indoors and allowing the

trees and plants around the perimeter to become part of the internal living space. Glass is also used to 'dematerialize' a structure, making it, or at least the obvious elements of its structure, melt away into the background. This is achieved with oversized glass doors that slide or fold away, creating a house that can be transformed into an open-air pavilion.

Brick, a material we often associate more with industrial or urban environments, has a complementary effect on an overgrown patio or outdoor shower, where a scattering of moss only adds

to its appeal. Even tile loses its mundane aspect and becomes more exciting in the sun-filled spaces of the tropics. And metal, seemingly impervious to conditions of light or damp that pervade the tropics, is also more flexible, varied and nature-friendly than one might think.

Almost any material, or indeed, combination of materials, can create a welcoming modern structure that fits well within, and takes advantage of, a prime location in the tropical landscape. It is the best and most innovative approaches that help appreciate every change in texture, colour and substance.

Wood

It has got to be nature's most versatile construction material. Used rough or polished, in planks or sheets, as a solid, structural element or lightweight decorative panel, wood imparts an awareness of substance and natural beauty. Opposite, the naturally weathered decking of this house on Sydney Harbour contrasts with the rich, red tones of the cedar screens that provide a protective layer to a bedroom terrace. Above, left to right, the grain of a natural wood table top is in sync with the other timber elements used in linear segments around the room; ventilation is key in a tropical interior, but this ceiling fan becomes a work of art, anchored to a grate made of timber slats against a polished wood ceiling; finely cut strips of wood enable this outdoor seating to curve as smoothly as a roll-top desk. The timber screen provides a sense of continuity, as well as privacy.

Tiles

The sybaritic pleasures of the luxury bathing space are enhanced with sweeping walls and floors of high-quality tiles. Impervious to water or damp, quarried tiles preserve the natural veins and variations in colour that reveal a geologic history, much like the rings of a tree present a natural timeline. Opposite, this selection of honey-coloured travertine in a house by Brisbane designer Elizabeth Watson Brown shows a wonderful variation in tone and pattern, revealing a kinship with the surrounding timber elements. Left, a bath area lined in slate, concrete and a subtle stone aggregate looks onto an external wall faced in a mosaic of river pebbles, creating a clean, neutral yet intriguing mix of textures and colour.

Mosaic tiles can sometimes feel commonplace, but in deeper hues, such as these ruby-toned glass tiles, opposite, they create a richly variegated block of colour, here in a space lit by a glass ceiling. Above left, more stretches of mosaic, this time on an external wall for a mid-century house in northwestern Brazil. The non-porous tiles make for resilient cladding in a climate of plentiful rain. Above right, variations in size and slightly irregular lines keep the glazed white tiles of this modern bath in a house by Donovan Hill in Brisbane from feeling overly uniform or clinical. The courtyard-style shower space introduces plenty of warm, natural light.

No matter where you are, natural stone has a profound effect on an interior, but in the tropics, the material has a particular allure. The weighty, potent essence of stone imparts an elemental quality, even to a contemporary building. Undressed stone on a living room hearth or shaped blocks on an outdoor terrace reinforce the indoor–outdoor atmosphere so identified with the tropics. Below, left and right, naturally variegated stone becomes part of a tactile decorative scheme. Opposite, the crisp, clean lines of glass, granite and steel in a modern Australian house are made to connect with the rougher textures of natural wood and rocky construction close by.

Stone

Glass

Advances in glass technology have made the indoor–outdoor dream a reality, even in less temperate parts of the world. In places where it is possible to open up a house to the air and sun for a good portion of the year, the conservatory style of outdoor living is not necessary. But those expansive sections of glass that keep internal temperatures comfortable can also be cast as doors that slide, pivot or fold back, so that any real barrier to the outside disappears. Opposite, a large sheet of glass wall makes the galley-style kitchen of this modern California house more expansive, as sliding doors open to the timber deck. Above, left to right, small panes of glass have a distinctive presence in this Brazilian apartment, giving it an Art Deco glamour; a single, uninterrupted glass surface gives an ethereal quality to a poolside view; and in the red sphere house in São Paulo, designed by Lucas Longo, sections of glass panes follow the curved form.

In addition to advances in thermal efficiency, there have also been huge technological improvements to the structural properties of glass, allowing for the construction of spaces that are free of any other supporting material. Above, left and right, a corner refuge in Sydney has a wondrous feeling of strength and fragility, while a series of pivoting glass doors is a good way to open up a living space to the garden when larger sections of glass are not possible. Opposite, louvred windows and tinted glass may have fallen out of favour with some designers, but the combination in this new angular design in Kuala Lumpur is artfully integrated with the colours of the pool and the clean geometry of the terrace.

09

Brick

Brick construction in tropical regions seems antithetical in some ways. Baked clay materials that degrade in wet weather do not seem the obvious choice for the climate. But as most inhabitants of inclement cities know, brick has an inherent breathable quality that allows it to take in quite a lot of moisture and dry out again. In the same way, brick can absorb heat, and cold, making it more robust than we might think. Opposite, an enchanting outdoor shower space in Bali welcomes a certain amount of natural intrusion. Above left, concrete in brick form creates a less monolithic structure than a single poured slab. Above middle, the natural variations in colour and tone of brick emphasize its organic quality. Above right, brick differs in colour depending on the type of clay used in its formation. This indoor–outdoor bathing area in a house near Kuala Lumpur takes its colour from the brick and outdoor planting.

Concrete

Contrary to what some would believe, concrete can be an incredibly warm and versatile material. While its place in the tropics is often associated with the bold, pure gestures of Oscar Niemeyer, it can also be used in more subtle or relaxed ways. Below left, concrete implies luxury in a single, smooth gesture, forming stair, walls and floor surface in a warm, pale hue. Below right, it takes on a more glamorous effect in a house in southern France, where a darker mix has been polished to a deep, reflective glow. Opposite, the home of a Los Angeles architect uses concrete to its best advantage in stark, sun-washed geometries.

09

Metal

Metal is another material that offers flexibility in all environments. Opposite, a house in Los Angeles by Anthony Coscia is an essay in the definition of space using light and materials. In the bathing area, corrugated metal panels open and close for privacy, and allow a view through the spaces. The hard surfaces of metal and tile set the space apart from the rest of the open-plan house. Above left, the radical design of Hugh Buhrich's house near Sydney includes a sculptural approach to materials, where a weathered metal shutter resembles a set of horizontal louvres in wood or leather. Above right, Coscia signals the serious business of cooking with an arrangement of stainless-steel units, set beneath a canopy roof.

Mixed-media

As wonderful as we may find any one material, few of us are unreserved purists when it comes to creating a living environment. In all, it is the careful mix of substance and texture that creates a sophisticated modern house. Above, concrete and stone, pebble and tile, timber and rock – a few examples of how minimal number of pure materials can be combined to ensure that each has an impact, but that doesn't overwhelm a house with a single tactile or tonal experience. Whatever material is the most prevalent in a tropical decor, glass or wood will probably be included for their respective qualities. Opposite, concrete, wood, metal, glass and tile are all used in this modern California house, but as each has a separate place and function, the result is a cool collaboration, rather than a confused mix.

Outdoors

The early modernist architects, like Rudolf Schindler and Richard Neutra, encouraged outdoor living, even though they each came from the cooler climates of Europe. Once they had moved to the subtropical regions of the US and Australia, however, these proponents of the International Style fully embraced the opportunities to create outdoor living spaces. The tropical house offers the enticement to live outdoors, but the really successful design is one that exploits the outside areas to make the most of the garden or landscape, giving these spaces as much prominence as the rooms inside.

Of course, the tropical climate has its limitations, being too warm for direct exposure outdoors in the high heat of a summer afternoon, or during the heavy storms that are part of the rainy season. And in a good modern design, these conditions are also accounted for in the application of shade and screens, wide porches, sheltered overhangs, cleverly placed pergolas, perhaps even a raised foundation to allow for the flow of rainwater. All of these practical considerations contribute to the basic success of the building, and to the quality of livable space, both inside and out.

As Geoffrey Bawa, probably Sri Lanka's most well-known architect, once put it, 'we have a marvellous tradition of building in this country that has got lost ... [architects] never built right "through" the landscape ... You must "run" with the site; after all, you don't want to push nature out with the building.' As much as this appears to advocate staunchly traditional styles of building, Bawa was a thorough modernist, and his best work shows the wonderful relationship between the modernist and the tropical environment. This is the thinking in a house that, to risk a cliché, is designed in harmony with

its natural environment, as so many good modern tropical houses are. And the best of these are made up of a combination of indoor and outdoor spaces that, though carefully designed, feel easy and welcoming.

The local vernacular of Sri Lanka, like many other tropical locales, encourages the inclusion of those outdoor areas that are so much a part of our ideal of the tropical house: courtyards or living areas that are, or can be, opened to the elements. In this chapter we look at the way these spaces can be exploited in the modern tropical context. We also look at wonderful examples of 'outdoor

rooms' with comfortable arrangements of elements and furnishings that make them more akin to interior spaces, so that there is almost no activity that cannot be enjoyed outside. We also look at elevated balconies, which can be much more than just a place to step outside and enjoy the view. And we look at paths and walkways, those areas of flow into and around the living spaces that can become enchanting garden experiences in themselves.

The great sense of freedom engendered by a house in the tropics comes out of the feeling that living

can happen without barriers, that people can move as happily through spaces as light and air. This happens naturally in mild climates, but in the well-designed modern house, the outdoor spaces are much more enriching than a bit of well-tended garden or patio; they are as essential to the life of the house as the traditional indoor living areas. Furnishings, materials and details are as important as the more common aspects, such as planting or light and shade. It's not about pushing nature out, but bringing it into everyday living.

A wide-open terrace or deck space, usually paved in some material that connects to the house, such as timber or even concrete, extends the life of the indoor spaces to the outside. It is a signal that welcomes people to carry themselves and their activities – eating, reading, relaxing – beyond the confines of the built structure. Below, left and right, an iconic modern house designed by Oscar Niemeyer was renovated and enhanced by a series of outdoor sitting areas at different levels on the backyard hillside. Below middle, another California house takes its cool modernism seriously, with immaculate outdoor spaces and classic modern furnishings. Opposite, the level pool deck corresponds to the pure geometry of the outdoor scheme, while an abundance of comfortable seating offers a softer corner of repose.

Terraces

Opposite, a house overlooking the idyllic sandy inlet of Palm Beach, north of Sydney, exploits its elevated position with a seamlessly glazed corner sitting room, bordered by a wraparound terrace with built-in seating. Below left, the living spaces of this Moroccan retreat are extended beyond and around the house by a surrounding terrace of massive, smooth paving stones. Below right, the changing levels and timber vocabulary of this New Zealand house have been carried through to the outdoor spaces, where terraces are covered in wood decking.

A small area for sitting out for a coffee or for arranging a few plants, a patio is usually a more intimate sheltered outdoor space that nevertheless offers ample opportunities for enjoying the natural setting. Opposite, the lush landscape of the Florida coast is very much a part of the life of this modern house. The small outdoor sitting area is one of several spots where the residents can enjoy the tropical surroundings. Below, left to right, a pretty outdoor arrangement in Sri Lanka; patterns of sunlight and shade, and a seating circle defined by creative paving and graduated greenery in a modernist classic in California. Following pages: a small patio arrangement is marked out from the larger terrace of an open, airy Moroccan home by a simple cluster of furnishings.

Patios

Gardens

In the tropics, the garden might be the whole, wide jungle, or it might be a small area of well-tended verdure that you have nurtured yourself. With such an array of exotic species to choose from, gardening in these climates may seem like an overwhelming proposition, but the really pleasurable tamed landscapes are those that feel both natural and well balanced. Above left, artful surprises are everywhere in artist Jean-François Fourtou's Moroccan retreat; outdoors they make an enchanted garden. Above right, ancient trees and old stone paving are a part of this captivating garden space in Sri Lanka. Opposite, a house designed by Geoffrey Bawa in Sri Lanka holds to his belief of integrating architecture with the site.

Opposite, for his holiday home in the South of France, fashion designer John Rocha created architectural elements for the garden that relate to the cool modern design of the house. But these work around elements of the existing landscape, such as the giant palms, while other smaller plantings have been added to blend and contrast with the stark, white insertions. Below, this garden of a modern Los Angeles house celebrates both gentle organization and abundance. The varied levels of the landscaped garden help create a more natural arrangement with the native plants, trees and shrubs.

Courtyards

There is something both highly civilized and slightly exotic about the courtyard garden. These are clandestine spaces that are also open; built rooms that are also outdoors and imbued with natural elements. Left, an Australian house built in clear, rectilinear modules includes the softening influence of a courtyard lawn. Opposite, the high walls of the courtyard garden leading from the living area of this house in São Paulo ensure a feeling of privacy, while allowing the residents to enjoy a very open-air living space in the middle of a highly populated area.

Opposite, while this house in Los Angeles includes a wide-open terrace with a swimming pool, the separate, enclosed courtyard provides an interim living area that is more protected from the high winds that come down along the hillsides. The glass wall allows for magnificent views in a peaceful semi-enclosure. Below left, a large enclosed garden area has more variation than the usual courtyard with changing levels and materials, a sculptural wall construction and swimming pool. Below right, making the most of a minimal internal courtyard space, the double-height plan wraps around the little enclosed lawn, while kitchen and living areas have space to overflow their boundaries.

The term has become something of a cliché, but it is still a highly prized amenity, to be able to have outdoor spaces that can function and feel as comfortable as your indoor furnished living areas. This is usually accomplished by having well-planned furniture arrangements (or built-ins) and putting thought into the position and views. Opposite, outdoor living in Bali seems effortless with only a few well-placed furnishings beneath a wide, sheltered porch overlooking a murmuring pool. Below, left to right, an oversized dining table in Brazil, an artful outdoor corner by artist Tomie Ohtake; and a backyard bar, complete with tall chairs, timber windscreen and decking.

Outdoor rooms

10

These California houses feature outdoor spaces
that are well designed and comfortable, but
their appeal lies in the way they have been
set into the natural vegetation, which creates
a secluded enclosure for lounging and
entertaining. Further planting and training
of vines and shrubs enhances the seating
area, opposite, and complements the wild
growth beyond.

The most inspiring garden designs offer a journey through the wonders of the natural landscape. This might be a meandering path through the surrounding forest, or a bit of interesting paving up the front walkway interspersed with some unusual native planting. Opposite, a simple route around the house takes a more interesting turn with paving broken up by sprouting lawn. Below left, regular blocks, woodchip covering and a black-painted timber wall make a zen-like arrangement in California. Below middle, the combination of neat pale surfaces and overhanging greenery emphasizes the integration of Modernism into nature in Brazil. Below right, more tidy lines of Modernism are carefully broken up by the natural landscape in this classic house by Oscar Niemeyer in Los Angeles. Following pages: further integration of modern geometry in nature in Brazil, left, and California, right.

Paths | walkways

Balconies

Too often balconies are small projections that only allow for minimal contact with the outdoors. In the modern tropical house, the balcony is an integral part of the plan, whether as part of a large bedroom terrace or an expanded living area, or just a place to sit comfortably and stare at the stars. Above, this Los Angeles house by Anthony Coscia defies conventional levels and boundaries. Its radical form creates a stepped balcony where a glass panel is used as safety rail, emphasizing the sense of transparency. Opposite, another unusual balcony in California features sheltered and exposed spaces, along with an outdoor bar area.

Opposite, avant-garde architect Hugh Buhrich's house near Sydney combines materials and forms that celebrate its association with the natural surroundings. This balcony seating area is positioned in the upper reaches of tall palms, with a view over the water. Below left, an apartment balcony in Sri Lanka makes the most of minimal space, with white-painted surfaces and a rattan lounger creating a comfortable, tree-shaded aerie. Below right, on the outskirts of Sydney, a multi-level house corresponds with the rising hillside setting. The lower-lovel balcony seems to float amid the trees and giant boulders.

10

Directory

49 Group
81 Sukhumvit 26
Bangkok 10110, Thailand
www.a49.com
27, 60, 98, 144, 152, 171

Marcos Acayaba
São Paulo, Brazil
www.marcosacayaba.arq.br
7, 35–36, 37, 131, 141

Architectus
Level 2, 3–13 Shortland Street
Auckland 1010, New Zealand
Level 4, 79 Adelaide Street
Brisbane, Queensland 4000, Australia
Level 7, 250 Victoria Parade
East Melbourne, Victoria 3002, Australia
Level 3, 341 George Street
Sydney, New South Wales 2000, Australia
www.architectus.com.au
157, 169

Area Designs
www.areadesigns.com
33, 45, 54, 118, 211, 222, 242, 243, 272

Andres Ariza, MXA Development
www.redbarnprefab.com, www.mxadevelopment.com
91, 101, 107, 161

Geoffrey Bawa
www.geoffreybawa.com
26, 62, 63, 82, 102, 215, 254–55, 265

Bedmar & Shi Architects
12a Keong Saik Road
Singapore 089119
www.bedmar-and-shi.com
248

Bestor Architecture
3920 Fountain Avenue
Los Angeles, California 90029, USA
www.bestorarchitecture.com
161, 176, 177, 205, 207, 245, 250

Blackman Cruz
836 North Highland Avenue
Los Angeles, California 90038, USA
www.blackmancruz.com
58, 61, 94, 110, 119, 180, 186

Bloc Design
Studio A, 4 Bay Street
Southport, Queensland 4215, Australia
www.blocdcl.com
169, 253

Boyd Design
www.boyddesign.com
4¬–5, 47, 70–71, 156, 172, 190, 191, 192–93, 252, 256, 261, 277, 279

Bricault Design
407 West Cordova Street
Vancouver, British Columbia V6B 1E5, Canada
www.bricault.ca
37, 140, 145, 161, 222

Casey Brown Architecture
East Sydney, New South Wales, Australia
www.caseybrown.com.au
215

Elizabeth Watson Brown Architects
www.elizabethwatsonbrownarchitects.com.au
28–29, 78, 233

Duangrit Bunnag Architect
www.dbalp.com
20–21, 86, 175, 240

Chang Architects
16 Morse Road, Unit 216
Singapore 099228
www.changarch.com
76, 80, 98, 130, 134, 181

Chu + Gooding Architects
2020 North Main Street, Suite 013
Los Angeles, California 90031, USA
www.cg-arch.com
145

Stephen Collins Design
www.scid.com.au
9

Commune Design
650 North Robertson Boulevard
Los Angeles California 90069, USA
www.communedesign.com
41, 50, 121, 132, 146, 202, 271, 273, 274, 276

George Cooper
Kahanda Kanda
Angulugaha, Galle, Sri Lanka
www.kahandakanda.com
18, 26, 109, 112

Coscia Day Architecture & Design
12732 Maxella Avenue
Los Angeles, California 90066, USA
www.cosciaday.com, www.skywavehouse.com
80, 124, 134, 147, 154, 182, 246, 247, 280

CSA Architects
185 Old South Head Road
Bondi Junction, New South Wales 2022, Australia
www.csa-arch.com.au
144

Wallace E. Cunningham
www.wallacecunningham.com
44, 74–75, 129, 135, 229

Giovanni d'Ercole
Shop 61, Level 1, Strand Arcade, Pitt Street Mall
Sydney, New South Wales 2000, Australia
www.loveandhatred.com.au
106, 110, 222

Design King
Unit 102, 21 Alberta Street
Sydney, New South Wales 2000, Australia
www.designking.com.au
6, 9, 40, 41, 113, 121, 145, 150, 190, 221, 229, 240, 258

Tony Duquette
P.O. Box 69858
West Hollywood, California 90069, USA
www.tonyduquette.com
114, 186, 215, 222

The Dutch House
18 Upper Dickson Road
Galle, Sri Lanka
www.thedutchhouse.com
17, 51, 130, 150, 186

Charles and Ray Eames
www.eamesfoundation.org, www.eamesoffice.com
111

Jack and Jo Eden
65A Lighthouse Street
Fort, Galle, Sri Lanka
www.villasinsrilanka.com, www.mimimango.com
94, 184, 207, 261

Ehrlich Architects
10865 Washington Boulevard
Culver City, California 90232, USA
www.s-ehrlich.com
68, 253

Marcelo Ferraz
Rua Harmonia, 101, Vila Madalena
São Paulo 05435 000, Brazil
www.brasilarquitetura.com
96, 106, 162

Jean-François Fourtou
www.jgmgalerie.com, www.harem-escape.com
7, 178, 207, 216, 218, 264

Sharon Fraser Architects
www.sharonfraserarchitects.com.au
6, 32, 87, 119, 268

Gordon & Valich Architects
Level 2, 105 Reservoir Street
Surry Hills, Sydney 2010, Australia
www.gordonvalich.com.au
31

Esther Gutmer Architecte d'Interieur
Rue des Pères blancs, 12
1040 Brussels, Belgium
www.esthergutmer.be
7, 46, 48–49, 54, 189, 190, 208, 219, 224, 244, 259, 262–63

Gerrad Hall Architects
103 Jervois Road
Herne Bay, Auckland, New Zealand
www.gerradhallarchitects.co.nz
8, 91, 98, 128, 243, 259

Hamilton Design Associates
One Union Square West, Suite 709
New York, New York 10003, USA
www.hdanyc.com
87, 248

Alexandre Herchcovitch
www.herchcovitch.uol.com.br
188, 200, 213, 217, 235, 277

Donovan Hill
112 Bowen Street
Spring Hill, Brisbane 4000, Australia
www.donovanhill.com.au
22, 80, 118, 125, 126, 196, 199, 235, 253

Kerry Hill Architects
29 Cantonment Road
Singapore 089746
30 Mouat Street
Fremantle, Western Australia 2962
www.kerryhillarchitects.com
41, 79, 109, 119

Aleks Istanbullu Architects
1659 11th Street, Suite 200
Santa Monica, California 90404, USA
www.ai-architects.com
105, 137

JAA Studio
Level 1, 105 Reservoir Street
Surry Hills, New South Wales 2010, Australia
www.jaastudio.com.au
12, 153, 203, 230, 231, 236

JMA Architects
17 Creswell Street
Newstead, Brisbane 4006, Australia
www.jma-arch.com
114

Jones Sonter Architects
505 Balmain Road, Lilyfield
Rozelle, New South Wales 2039, Australia
www.jonesonter.com.au
167

JPRA Architects
39300 West Twelve Mile Road, Suite 180
Farmington Hills, Michigan 48331, USA
www.jpra.com
88, 166, 177, 182, 214, 239

Kappe + Du Architects
801 D Street
San Rafael, California 94901, USA
www.kappedu.com
9, 14–15, 23, 66, 106, 127, 168, 226

Carole Katleman Interiors
carolekatleman@roadrunner.com
68, 228

Picture references

Key:
• Location is given, followed by the principal designer or architect, or owner. Designers and architects are also listed on pp. 284–85.
• All images listed from left to right, unless otherwise indicated.

1 Australia / Frank Macchia Architect
2–3 Brazil / Eduardo Longo
4–5 California, USA / Boyd Design
6 Australia / Sharon Fraser Architects; Australia / Janet Charlton; Sri Lanka / MICD Architects; Australia / Design King
7 Morocco / Esther Gutmer Architecte d'Interieur; Brazil / Marcos Acayaba; Morocco / Jean-François Fourtou; Malaysia / Seksan Design; New Zealand / Warren & Mahoney
8 Brazil / Paulo Mendes da Rocha; Singapore / SCDA Architects; New Zealand / Gerrad Hall Architects
9 Australia / Stephen Collins Design, Design King; California, USA / Kappe + Du Architects; Singapore / SCDA Architects; California, USA / Techentin Buckingham Architecture

10 Malaysia / Seksan Design
12 California, USA / Marmol Radziner; Sri Lanka / Laki Senanayake; Australia / JAA Studio
13 Australia / Tim Roberts Design; Sri Lanka / Anjalendran; Malaysia / Seksan Design
14–15 California, USA / Kappe + Du Architects
16 Australia / Greg Lamond; Australia / Robertson & Hindmarsh Architects
17 Sri Lanka / The Dutch House
18 (top row, left to right) California, USA / Marmol Radziner; Australia / Tonkin Zulaikha Greer Architects; California, USA / Standard; (bottom row, left to right) California, USA / Frank Lloyd Wright, Jr; Sri Lanka / George Cooper; Brazil / Studio MK27
19 California, USA / Marmol Radziner
20–21 Thailand / Duangrit Bunnag Architect
22 Australia / Donovan Hill
23 Australia / Tonkin Zulaikha Greer Architects; California, USA / Kappe + Du Architects; Brazil / Isay Weinfeld
24 Brazil / Isay Weinfeld
24–25 Brazil / Studio Arthur Casas
26 Sri Lanka / Geoffrey Bawa; Sri Lanka / George Cooper; Brazil / Studio Arthur Casas
27 Thailand / 49 Group
28–29 Australia / Elizabeth Watson Brown Architects
29 Thailand / Spacetime Architecture & Interior Design
30 California, USA / Marmol Radziner
31 Australia / Gordon & Valich Architects
32 Australia / Sharon Fraser Architects
33 Bali / Area Designs
34–35 Brazil / Marcos Acayaba
36 Australia / Hugh Buhrich Architect
37 (top row, left to right) Brazil / Isay Weinfeld; Brazil / Paulo Mendes da Rocha; California, USA / Sebastian Mariscal Studio; (bottom row, left to right) California, USA / Bricault Design; Brazil / Eduardo Longo; Brazil / Marcos Acayaba

38 Brazil / Isay Weinfeld
40 Australia / Design King; Australia / Tim Roberts Design
41 Australia / Design King; Singapore / Kerry Hill Architects; California, USA / Commune Design
42–43 Brazil / Isay Weinfeld
44 California, USA / Wallace E. Cunningham
45 Bali / Area Designs
46 Morocco / Esther Gutmer Architecte D'Interieur
47 Rudy Ricciotti Architecte; California, USA / Boyd Design; Brazil / Isay Weinfeld
48–49 Morocco / Esther Gutmer Architecte d'Interieur

50 Sri Lanka / MICD Architects; California, USA / Commune Design
51 Sri Lanka / The Dutch House
52 Australia / Luigi Rosselli Architects
53 California, USA / Marmol Radziner
54 Morocco / Esther Gutmer Architecte d'Interieur; Bali / Area Designs; California, USA / Steve Shaw
55 France / John Rocha
56 California, USA / Lorcan O'Herlihy Architects
57 Florida, USA / Toshiko Mori Architect; Brazil / Studio MK27
58 Malaysia / Seksan Design; California, USA / Blackman Cruz
59 New Zealand / Andrew Lister Architect
60 Thailand / 49 Group
61 Singapore / WoHa Architects; California, USA / Sebastian Mariscal Studio; California, USA / Blackman Cruz
62 Sri Lanka / Geoffrey Bawa
63 Sri Lanka / Geoffrey Bawa (left and middle); Sri Lanka / Laki Senanayake
64–65 Sri Lanka / Laki Senanayake

66 California, USA / Kappe + Du Architects
68 California, USA / Ehrlich Architects; Brazil / Studio Arthur Casas; California, USA / Carole Katleman Interiors
69 California, USA / Sebastian Mariscal Studio; France / John Rocha
70–71 California, USA / Boyd Design
72 Australia / Suzanne & Kris
73 Brazil / Isay Weinfeld (left and right); Brazil / Studio Arthur Casas
74–75 California, USA / Wallace E. Cunningham
75 Brazil / Isay Weinfeld
76 California, USA / Standard; Singapore / Chang Architects
77 California, USA / Standard
78 Australia / Elizabeth Watson Brown Architects
79 California, USA / Marmol Radziner; Singapore / Kerry Hill Architects
80 (top row, left to right) Australia / Tonkin Zulaikha Greer Architects; Singapore / Chang Architects; California, USA / Coscia Day Architecture and Design; (bottom row, left to right) California, USA / Coscia Day Architecture and Design; Australia / Donovan Hill; California, USA / Techentin Buckingham Architecture
81 Australia / Tonkin Zulaikha Greer Architects
82 Sri Lanka / Geoffrey Bawa
83 California, USA / Frank Lloyd Wright, Jr
84–85 Brazil / Studio Arthur Casas
86 Thailand / Duangrit Bunnag Architect
87 (top row, left to right) Australia / Sharon Fraser Architects; California, USA / Trina Turk; (middle row, left to right) France / Rudy Ricciotti Architecte; California, USA / Hamilton Design Associates; (bottom row, left to right) California, USA / Standard; California, USA / Sebastian Mariscal Studio
88 Brazil / JPRA Architects; Australia / Tony Owen Partners
89 Brazil / Studio Arthur Casas
90 California, USA / Greg Lynn FORM
91 (top row, left to right) California, USA / Andres Ariza - MXA Development; New Zealand / Gerrad Hall Architects; (bottom row, left to right) California, USA / Techentin Buckingham Architecture; Singapore / Studio Daminato
92 Brazil / Studio MK27
94 Sri Lanka / Jack and Jo Eden; California, USA / Blackman Cruz; California, USA / Techentin Buckingham Architecture
95 Sri Lanka / Anjalendran; Sri Lanka / Olivia Richli; California, USA / Techentin Buckingham Architecture
96 Brazil / Marcelo Ferraz
97 Singapore / SCDA Architects; Brazil / Isay Weinfeld
98 (top row, left to right) New Zealand / Gerrad Hall Architects; Singapore / WoHa Architects; Australia / Elizabeth Leong Architect; (bottom row, left to right)

Thailand / 49 Group; Brazil / Isay Weinfeld; Singapore / Chang Architects
99 Brazil / Eduardo Longo
100 California, USA / Greg Lynn, FORM
101 France / John Rocha (left and middle); California, USA / Andres Ariza, MXA Development
102 Sri Lanka / Geoffrey Bawa; Brazil / Isay Weinfeld
103 Brazil / Studio Arthur Casas
104 California, USA / Trina Turk; California, USA / Techentin Buckingham Architecture
105 California, USA / Aleks Istanbullu Architects
106 (top row, left to right) Australia / Giovanni d'Ercole; California, USA / Kappe + Du Architects; California, USA / Sebastian Mariscal Studio; (bottom row, left to right) Brazil / Marcelo Ferraz; Australia / Frank Macchia Architect; California, USA / Greg Lynn, FORM
107 California, USA / Andres Ariza - MXA Development
108 Brazil / Studio MK27
109 Singapore / Kerry Hill Architects; Sri Lanka / George Cooper; Brazil / Eduardo Longo
110 (top row, left to right) California, USA / Blackman Cruz; Australia / Giovanni d'Ercole; (bottom row, left to right) California, USA / Blackman Cruz; Brazil / Isay Weinfeld
111 California, USA / The Eames Foundation (eamesfoundation.org) and Eames Office, LLC (eamesoffice.com)
112 Sri Lanka / George Cooper
113 Australia / Design King
114 (top row, left to right) Brazil / Studio MK27; Australia / JMA Architects; Singapore / WoHa Architects; (bottom row, left to right) Sri Lanka / MICD Architects; California, USA / Tony Duquette; Brazil / Eduardo Longo
115 Australia / Kidd & Co Designers

116 Brazil / Studio Arthur Casas
118 Australia / Donovan Hill; Bali / Area Designs; Brazil / Eduardo Longo
119 Australia / Sharon Fraser Architects; Singapore / Kerry Hill Architects; California, USA / Blackman Cruz
120 California, USA / Marmol Radziner
121 Australia / Design King; California, USA / Commune Design
122–23 Brazil / Isay Weinfeld
124 California, USA / Coscia Day Architecture and Design
125 Sri Lanka / Anjalendran; Brazil / Studio Arthur Casas; Australia / Donovan Hill
126 Australia / Donovan Hill
127 California, USA / Kappe + Du Architects
128 New Zealand / Gerrad Hall Architects
129 California, USA / Wallace E. Cunningham
130 (top row, left to right) Australia / Hugh Buhrich Architect; Brazil / Studio MK27; Australia / JAA Studio; (bottom row, left to right) Sri Lanka / The Dutch House; Brazil / Rodrigo Bueno; Singapore / Chang Architects
131 Brazil / Marcos Acayaba
132 California, USA / Lorcan O'Herlihy Architects; California, USA / Commune Design; Brazil / Eduardo Longo
133 Brazil / Isay Weinfeld
134 California, USA / Coscia Day Architecture and Design; Singapore / Chang Architects
135 California, USA / Wallace E. Cunningham
136–37 Brazil / Ruy Ohtake
137 California, USA / Aleks Istanbullu Architects
138 California, USA / Marmol Radziner
139 Brazil / Studio Arthur Casas; Australia / Robertson & Hindmarsh Architects
140 California, USA / Bricault Design; Sri Lanka / Anjalendran; California, USA / Greg Lynn, FORM
141 Brazil / Marcos Acayaba

142 Australia / Frank Macchia Architect
144 Australia / CSA Architects; Thailand / 49 Group; California, USA / Techentin Buckingham Architecture
145 California, USA / Kay Kollar Design, Chu + Gooding Architects; California, USA / Bricault Design; Australia / Design King

For Maximilian

Over the years I have been given access to the most
amazing homes all over the world, so a huge thanks goes
to the homeowners, architects and designers for their
part in *Living Modern Tropical*.

A special thanks to all the writers, stylists and producers
with whom I have collaborated, including Dominic
Bradbury, Georgie Bean, Graca Buena, Amanda Talbot,
Jean Wright, David Robson, Alison Gee, Tami Christiansen,
Justine Osbourne, Margie Fraser, Karen McCartney,
David Harrison and Michael Webb.

Particular thanks are due to my wife Danielle, whose
productions feature throughout this book.

Thanks also to Phyllis Richardson and Anna Perotti, as
well as Lucas Dietrich, Elain McAlpine and Sadie Butler at
Thames & Hudson for their tremendous teamwork; and to
the editors and staff of the magazines around the world for
their continuing support of my work.